LET'S START WEANING

LET'S START WEANING

An explicit cookbook for your baby's food

SANYA MOIZ

Copyright © 2022 by Sanya Moiz

All rights reserved. No part of this book may be reproduced or used in any manner without the prior written permission of the copyright owner except for the use of quotations in a book review. For more information, address: mom4amdoha@gmail.com

FIRST EDITION

www.mom4amdoha@gmail.com

978-1-80227-372-4 (eBook)
978-1-80227-373-1 (paperback)
978-1-80227-374-8 (hard cover)

Contents

Meet Sanya and Zia! 1

FOUNDATION

Baby's first diet	5
Nutritional requirements	8
Children's food pyramid	17
Portion size for every meal	25
Foods to avoid and allergenic foods	27
Plot and plan	36
Dealing with fussy eaters	45
How to cut food for baby-led weaning	49
Equipment/tools needed	51
Cooking terms	53
The ingredients your kitchen needs	58
Basic cooking measurement conversions	61
Storing and thawing baby food	63

Contents

STRUCTURE

LEVEL 1 – 6 MONTHS TO 7 MONTHS

First foods - Purées 67

Schematic weekly planner (6 months to 7 months)

LEVEL 2 – 7 MONTHS TO 9 MONTHS

First foods to finger foods 75

Purées 77

Breakfast 103

Schematic weekly planner (7 months to 9 months+)

LEVEL 3 – 9 MONTHS TO 12 MONTHS AND BEYOND

Finger food to table food 119

Breakfast 121

Main course 163

Snacks and drinks 225

Treats 267

Schematic weekly planner (9 months to 12 months+)

Acknowledgments	291
Index of recipes	292
About the author	296

Dedicated to my son, Zia.

Meet Sanya and Zia

Hello everyone,

I'm an expatriate mom living in Qatar. My life revolves around my family and friends, especially my son, Zia, who is handsome and friendly. He is two years old and a hyperactive and curious toddler. I started weaning Zia, with the approval of my pediatrician, when he was 5 months old. I opted for the spoon-feeding method, and his very first food was a mashed banana. Initially, he liked purées for about a month, then suddenly he started rejecting my purées. I tried homemade, store-bought, organic; I tried everything, and he turned his nose up at them all. Did I have the fussiest child on earth? I was at my wits' end. I think every mom (parent) would be worried if their child stopped eating completely, wouldn't they?

Meet Sanya and Zia

Coming from a traditional Pakistani household, I wasn't exposed to as many international flavors as some people are. This might have contributed to my being a slightly picky eater later in life. I didn't want Zia to be a picky eater like me. I wanted to reinforce healthy eating habits, instill an appreciation for an array of tastes, and let him explore the world of food.

One night, I was surfing the internet, worried and exhausted as I hadn't been able to wean him for a month. Scrolling through the pages, I came across an intriguing article on "baby-led weaning". It was the first time I had heard about "finger foods". Desperate as I was, and still having reservations about the possible choking/gagging hazards, I started practicing baby-led weaning (BLW). The very next day, I made French toast and cut it into fingers, and to my amazement, he loved it! I could see Zia was enjoying touching the food, feeling its texture, and reacting to its color and smell, and seeing him express a newfound sense of independence filled me with pride.

From the start of my weaning adventure, I recognized how important it was to establish positive eating habits for Zia. The first two years of a child's life are crucial for reinforcing healthy eating habits and establishing a foundation for a healthy diet. It is of foremost importance for parents to let their babies explore the diversity of nutritious food.

Meet Sanya and Zia

I have divided the book into two main parts:

FOUNDATION, which is the core knowledge of weaning and includes a complete handbook for first-time parents or anyone who is having a hard time weaning their baby.

STRUCTURE, which includes over 100 recipes and schematic meal planners for your kids from 6 months and beyond.

This book represents a great accomplishment for me as I'd never dreamed of writing a short story, never mind a complete cookbook. This book will guide you all the way through your weaning journey, and I hope going through this book will provide you and your baby with many happy weaning memories.

So, shall we start?

Are you ready?

Let the weaning begin.

Foundation

Baby's first diet

Milk

The American Academy of Pediatrics (AAP) recommends feeding babies only breast/formula milk for the first 6 months of life. After that, the AAP recommends a combination of solid foods and breast/formula milk until a baby is at least 1 year old. Then, babies may begin drinking whole cow's milk. In fact, the World Health Organization (WHO) recommends that moms breastfeed for the first 2 years of a child's life.

I encourage moms to breastfeed their babies if they have the opportunity as breast milk

From 6 months onwards, a small quantity of cow's milk can be added to baby's cooked meals, such as pancakes and French toasts.

contains antibodies that can shield their baby from becoming sick and protect against allergies and obesity. It provides nutrients in the proper ratio. It is easily digested, and babies have fewer chances of developing constipation and diarrhea.

What is weaning?

Weaning is when a baby is offered additional nourishment to breast/formula milk as part of their transitioning to a normal diet.

When to start weaning?

Most moms are concerned about the right time to wean. According to WHO, around the age of 6 months, an infant's immune system is well-developed and they need more nutrients and energy than breast/formula milk can provide.

WHO recommends that infants start complementary foods at 6 months of age, on top of breast/formula milk. Initially, they should receive complementary foods 2–3 times a day between 6 and 8 months and increase to 3–4 times daily between 9 and 24 months. Additional nutritious snacks should also be offered 1–2 times per day for ages 12–24 months, as desired.

Complementary feeding typically covers the period from 6–24 months of age, even though breastfeeding may continue till two years of age.

Signs of readiness:

- Holds his neck properly.
- Can sit upright with or without support.
- Opens his mouth in anticipation during feeding.
- Swallows or sucks food instead of spitting it out.
- Coordinates his eye, hand, and mouth to look at the food, pick it up, and put it into his mouth by himself.

Nutritional requirements

Nutrients are required by a baby to maintain development and prevent illness. The dietary facts below will help you to prepare your kid's meals according to their requirements.

Fluids

As previously mentioned, breast/formula milk is a baby's first drink. Other fluids are to be given only after 6 months because infants have tiny tummies and they fill up rapidly. Their kidneys aren't well developed so cannot process other fluids such as water. However, water can be added to an infant's diet from 6 months onwards.

> After weaning has begun, the primary source of a baby's food is still breast/formula milk till 12 months.
>
> Human beings are made up of 60% water by weight.

Nutritional requirements

Water is the best drink for your babies from 6 months onwards. It can be served along with meals. Avoid giving store-bought infant fruit juices to your babies as they have a high sugar content which often leads to poor oral health, weight gain, and the development of a sweet palate. Fresh, homemade juice diluted with 8 to 10 times the amount of water could be better to serve to kids under 12 months.

According to Community Paediatric Review (CPR), "The daily fluid intake for children 0–12 months old should be around 150ml/kg. After 6 months, a portion of this fluid is provided by solids, and it is normal for fluid intake to decrease. Children 1 – 5 years old should drink at least one liter each day. This includes water, milk in cereal, and juice."

Beware of weather and activities. Toddlers don't ask for water when they get thirsty, so encourage them to drink water after every 20 to 40 minutes to prevent dehydration. Limit the water during mealtimes because it might fill your child's tiny tummy.

*See your pediatric ian before starting fluids, especially before 6 months.

For healthy summer drinks, see page 244.

Macronutrients

Macronutrients such as carbohydrates, proteins, and fats are the basic energy-giving components of a meal. Kids get most of their energy from these macronutrients, so including them in your baby's meals will provide the energy they need to play and help them to grow.

Carbohydrates

Carbohydrates are the major source of energy for our kids. Carbs are found in a wide range of foods, such as rice, cereals, lentils, potatoes, berries, apples, yogurt, fizzy drinks, and sweets. Carbohydrates should be added to every kid's meal in a certain quantity, but make sure you choose wisely. Cookies, candy bars, and sodas also contain carbohydrates and should be limited to tiny quantities and served only occasionally.

Carbohydrates include complex carbs and simple carbs. Complex carbs are mostly starchy foods and are known as dietary fiber. Most carbohydrates metabolize to glucose (sugar) that is the primary oxidative fuel for the brain. For example, when kids have a slice of bread, it releases energy in their bodies that they can use. And when we choose to serve brown rice over white rice, we will increase the amount of fiber that is consumed. This is great for a kid's health and will also prevent them from getting hungry again too quickly.

Dietary Fiber

Fiber, also called roughage, is an important part of the diet. However, it is the indigestible part of plant foods that the digestive tract can't break down and absorb. It protects the health of the digestive tract and helps prevent constipation as it aids in removing waste from the body.

Proteins

I'm confident you all know that proteins provide some energy and help to repair and maintain the growth of children's bodies, but proteins also play a whole bunch of other important roles. For example, when kids get sick, their immune system is activated, and proteins boost their immune reaction. Proteins act as a transporter in a variety of different roles, such as maintaining the right fluid distribution in the body.

Proteins are made up of different amino acids, but 9 of them are called essential because they are obtained from the foods we eat. Animal sources of protein (eggs, chicken, red meat, and fish) tend to be complete and contain all essential amino acids in sufficient amounts to support the growth, repair, and maintenance of our kids' bodies. That means that when kids consume a boiled egg or an omelet in the morning, they will get all 9 essential amino acids for growth and repairing their bodies.

Dairy products (milk, cheese, and yogurt) are also good sources of protein, and there are many vegetable sources of protein such as tofu, beans, pulses, and nuts, but dairy and vegetarian sources of protein tend to be incomplete. But then there is a trick: if you combine vegetarian-sourced protein with certain other foods, such as Indian dal (pulses), Mexican beans, and rice, you may end up with a meal that provides a complete set of amino acids.

Fats

Dietary fats provide a large amount of energy and are important for the healthy growth and development of our babies. Most importantly, they are essential for brain enhancement and the development of the nervous system. Dietary fats help our bodies to absorb vitamins, and they're the building blocks of hormones. Furthermore, when our child consumes a meal that has a certain amount of fat in it, they're less likely to feel hungry soon after the meal. Fats slow down the speed at which glucose or sugar is released into the blood, so they regulate the blood sugar level in the body.

> Try to minimize using oil in cooking; you can use butter or olive oil.

Dietary fats are divided into two main categories:

- **Saturated fats, such as butter and animal fat**, are usually solid at room temperature, which may lead to high cholesterol and arterial plaques later in life.

- **Unsaturated fats** are further divided into two kinds, natural unsaturated fats, and man-made unsaturated fats.

Naturally occurring unsaturated fats are usually liquid at room temperature and are found in vegetable oils such as olive oil. The oils in nuts are also quite rich in unsaturated fats.

Man-made saturated fats are found in margarine or in cooking oil that has been used over and over again. Man-made fats are often chemically altered, which leads to the creation of two trans fats that tend to increase bad cholesterol and reduce the good cholesterol in the body.

Micronutrients

Micronutrients include vitamins and minerals that a body needs to grow, repair, and function normally.

Vitamins

Various types of vitamins play their part in the growth and development of children's bodies. They also help to maintain their immune system. Fruits and veggies are a significant source of vitamins, so be sure to include 2 to 3 servings of fruit and veggies in your kid's meals every day. When it comes to vitamins, each one has a special role to play:

Vitamin A strengthens vision (particularly night vision) and promotes healthy skin.

Vitamin B provides energy to the body.

Vitamin C maintains body tissues, heals wounds, and is important for the development of the body.

Vitamin D maintains strong bones and teeth. Young children don't get enough vitamin D, and in winter, babies need to take vitamin D in drops or liquid form* every day.

*Consult your doctor for the quantity.

Fruits and veggies are the best sources of vitamin C, also known as ascorbic acid. However, the amount of this important vitamin may be reduced by prolonged storage and by cooking because ascorbic acid is water-soluble and can be destroyed by heat. Steaming or microwaving may lessen cooking losses. Fortunately, many of the best food sources of vitamin C, such as fruits and vegetables, are usually consumed raw or not overly cooked.

Minerals

Minerals include calcium, iron, zinc, sodium, and potassium and are essential for development and good health. They are found in the earth and in food. A balanced diet provides a complete range of all the essential minerals for your baby.

Calcium

According to The International Foundation for Mother and Child Health, the daily calcium intake for a 6-month-old baby should be at least 500 mg. Most of the time, the calcium requirements are fulfilled through formula milk or breast milk. Calcium helps to develop strong bones and teeth. You can add calcium to your baby's diet by giving him full-fat dairy products such as yogurt, milk, and cheese, as well as calcium-rich foods such as orange juice and oatmeal.

Iron

Normally, babies are born with enough iron reserves to last them for four to five months. However, according to the International Foundation for Mother and Child, after the initial 4-5 months, their diet needs to be supplemented with 11 mg of iron daily. Iron helps in producing hemoglobin and providing an adequate amount of oxygen to the heart. Iron also has a vital role to play in improving memory and the development of the brain. Foods like spinach, soya beans, eggs, potatoes, and fortified cereals are rich in iron.

Foundation

Food and nutrient source chart

Let's have a look at what foods provide what nutrients:

- Whole grains and cereals
- Whole grain pasta
- Beans
- White and brown rice
- Whole fruits
- Potato, etc.

HEALTHY CARBS

- Meat
- Poultry
- Fish
- Lentils and beans
- Dairy, etc.

PROTEIN

- Avocado
- Olive oil
- Cheese
- Chia seeds
- Nuts, etc.

HEALTHY FATS

- Berries
- Whole corn
- Whole grains
- Apple
- Potato with skin, etc.

FIBER

- Milk (cow, almond, soya, etc.)
- Yogurt
- Cheese
- Dark green leafy veggies
- Dried beans, etc.

CALCIUM

- Red meat
- Beans, such as red kidney beans, edamame beans and chickpeas
- Nuts
- Dried fruit (dried apricots, etc.)

IRON

- Carrot
- Spinach
- Sweet potato
- Liver
- Dairy products, etc.

VITAMIN A

- Citrus fruits, avocado, banana
- Meat, poultry, fish
- Dairy products
- Dark leafy vegetables, etc.

VITAMIN B

- Yellow sweet pepper
- Chili pepper
- Citrus fruits
- Broccoli, kale, etc.

VITAMIN C

- Sunlight
- Salmon
- Mushrooms
- Egg yolks, etc.

VITAMIN D

- Butternut squash
- Broccoli
- Mango
- Cooking oil (wheat germ oil, sunflower oil, etc.)
- Peanut butter, etc.

VITAMIN E

Children's Food Pyramid

Let the children's food pyramid guide your choices

Being moms, we often get puzzled about the amount of food to serve or what food to give first to nourish our kids' bodies. Taking into consideration children's food pyramids from around the world could be helpful to fulfill our child's daily nutritional requirements.

The children's food pyramid found in the Irish Department of Health's leaflet is a guide to how much food to offer. These guidelines have been developed by nutrition experts in Ireland and are based on Irish and international evidence.

It is designed for two age groups:

- 1- and 2-year-old children
- 3- and 4-year-old children.

Foundation

The Children's Food Pyramid has six shelves. Each shelf shows:

- a variety of foods
- child-size servings

It is important to offer your child the number of servings suitable for their age, although, depending on their size/weight, they can eat less or more.

*The Children's Food Pyramid above shows examples of foods on each food shelf. It does not represent the amount of food a 1 to 4 year old child should eat every day.

Cereals, bread, potatoes, pasta, and rice

Cereals, bread, potatoes, pasta, and rice are on the biggest shelf of the Children's Food Pyramid. The reason for this is that children need these foods for energy and to grow. Starchy foods provide fiber and some vitamin B. Try to offer at least one of these foods at every meal, which will be converted into energy.

If your child is prone to constipation, offer more whole-meal and wholegrain varieties. Make sure they eat vegetables and drink enough fluid. Fiber-rich foods help to remove waste from the body.

Offer your child breakfast cereal with added iron most days of the week. This is especially important for younger children.

While many parents will opt for whole-meal/wholegrain options as their health benefits are well known, these foods can also be overly filling and could reduce your child's appetite for other nourishing foods. Young children can meet their fiber needs by having a mix of white and whole-meal cereals and bread. Having this mix will still leave room for other food groups.

Adjust these servings to suit your child. Smaller, younger children will eat less. Taller, older, and more active children will eat more. Each of these examples shows 1- and 2-year-olds can have 2, 3 or 4 servings a day. 3- and 4-year-olds can have 3 to 6 servings a day.

Vegetables, salad, and fruits

These foods act as an essential source of vitamins, minerals, and fiber. That is why they are on the second shelf of the Children's Food Pyramid. Try to offer a variety of freshly chopped veggies and fruit in every meal and snack.

An average serving size is about 40g. A serving size that fits into half the pallm of your hand is about right for children aged 1 to 4.

As I mentioned above, vitamin C is water-soluble and it is destroyed by prolonged storage and being overcooked. Therefore, offer fruits and vegetables raw or not excessively cooked. Furthermore, steaming vegetables and fruits might help preserve more nutrients.

Milk, yogurt, and cheese

Dairy products develop strong bones and teeth. Offering milk as a drink with meals is an easy way to give your child one of the three daily servings they need. A small pot of plain or natural fromage frais is a good option to serve with meals or snacks.

> Limit dried fruits to once a week because:
> - they contain sugar
> - they are sticky
> - they are not kind to teeth.

It does not include foods made from milk that have little calcium and a high fat content, such as cream cheese, sour cream, cream, and butter.

> Breastmilk counts towards these servings. Breastfeeding mothers can add cow's milk to their 1-year-old's cereal or offer cow's milk as a drink. It is important to include yogurt and cheese as well to help meet your child's nutritional needs.

Non-dairy soya "milk" can be offered if your child is allergic to cow's milk or lactose intolerant. These should be unsweetened and fortified with calcium.

Skimmed milk is not suitable for kids under 5. Offer full-fat milk to kids under 2. However, you can offer low-fat milk to kids who are over 3, or it can be given earlier if your kid is overweight.

Meat, poultry, fish, eggs, beans, and nuts

These are the main sources of protein and also provide iron, which helps kids grow and develop. Offer meat, poultry, fish, eggs, beans, or nuts to your child at each of their 2 main meals every day. Try to avoid giving processed meat such as bacon and sausages. Limit these to once a week in exceedingly small quantities.

Oily fish contains omega 3 and vitamin D. Some types of fish are good for children's brain and eye development so offer them once a week. Avoid giving shellfish or fish which are high in mercury because the amount of mercury in these fish can affect the development of a baby's nervous system.

Good vegetarian protein sources include:

- eggs
- soya products
- peas
- chickpeas
- beans
- nuts
- seeds

> Chicken nuggets, sausages, and burgers have less protein and are high in fat and salt. They should not be a regular part of your child's diet.

> Offer your child smooth nut butter without added sugar and salt. Whole nuts should not be given to children under 3 because of the risk of choking.

Protein is not a problem for vegetarian diets, but iron can be. Consult a registered dietitian for advice. Foods from the milk, yogurt, and cheese shelf also provide protein.

Fats, spreads, and oils

Whilst essential fats can be provided by all foods, spreads and oils are one area in which we can be in total control of the fats being offered. They should be healthy fats and used in small quantities.

Small quantity: 1 teaspoon of spread on bread.

½ teaspoon of oil for cooking.

Choose rapeseed, olive, canola, sunflower, or corn oils for cooking, but avoid mayonnaise and salad dressings containing too much oil.

Instead of frying food in fats and oil, you could do the following:

- Grill
- Steam
- Oven-bake
- Boil
- Stir-fry

The red triangle at the top of the Children's Food Pyramid

This is the least essential/nutritious part of the Children's Food Pyramid and contains foods such as fizzy drinks and crisps/chips that are high in fat, sugar, and salt. These are not nutritionally needed and should be given only occasionally to keep the child at a healthy weight.

Sweets, chocolates, biscuits, cakes, fizzy drinks, and chips shouldn't be part of a child's daily meal. Try to avoid these as much as you can during the early years of your child. They can be given once a week in TINY amounts.

TINY amount: one square of chocolate, half a biscuit, 3 chips, 3 soft sweets.

Takeaways can be high in fat and salt and should not be part of your child's diet.

Frozen pizza can be high in fat so limit it to a small slice once a week.

Sugary foods and drinks are not good for your child's teeth.

Portion size for every meal

Do you ever find yourself confused about how to create the right portion size and pack your kid's lunch boxes if they are going to daycare, kindergarten, or school?

"MyPlate" is something you should take into account. It is a nutrition guide from the United States Department of Agriculture, the USDA's Center of Nutrition Policy and Promotion, published in 2011. It is a visual representation of a single meal divided into 5 food groups – Fruits, Vegetables, Grains, Protein, and Dairy. It is designed to encourage children and adults to eat food in the correct proportions.

Myplate is divided into sections, and half of the plate is divided into fruits and vegetables. As you can see, it is suggested that the portion of vegetables should be slightly larger than that of fruits. The other half of the plate is divided into grains and protein, with grain being more

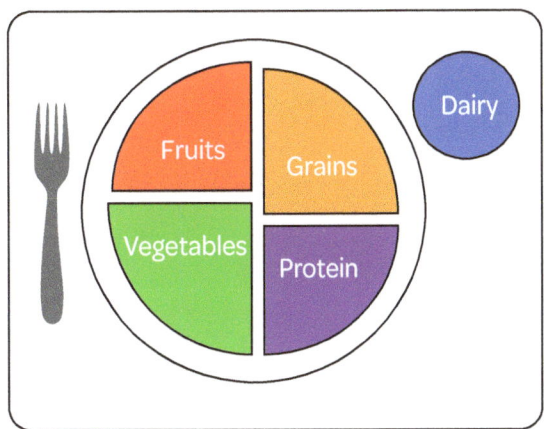

prominently represented than protein. The smaller circle represents the one serving of dairy products.

Encourage your kids to have a variety of food, including veggies and fruits, by making it colorful and fun. Below are some ideas for food preparation:

Fruits	Veggies	Grains	Protein	Dairy
You can choose whole fruits or 1 part fresh juice diluted with 8 parts of water	Choose green and orange veggies	Try to ensure that half of the grain is whole grain	Include low-sodium meat and low-mercury fish	Choose full-fat dairy products for kids under 2 years
apple	sweet potato	wholegrain bread	chicken	plain yogurt
banana	broccoli	cereal	lentils	milk
kiwifruit	carrot	brown rice	fish	cheese
strawberry	cauliflower	pasta	beans	milkshake
orange	zucchini	pita bread	nut butter	fromage frais
melon	red pepper	white rice	turkey/beef/mutton	flavored yogurt
peach	cucumber	breadsticks	peas	custard

Foods to avoid and allergenic foods

Do you know that there are a few foods you should avoid while weaning? Little tummies are still developing and some foodstuffs can harm their inner health.

Honey

Avoid giving honey to your baby till the baby is 12 months old. The reason for this is that honey contains bacteria that may cause infant botulism, an exceedingly rare but life-threatening illness. After 12 months, it should still be used only in moderation.

Salt

Baby's kidneys are too immature to cope with an excess amount of salt. Adding too much salt to a baby's food is harmful to their kidneys and it also leads to a lifelong preference for salty food that can jeopardize their future health. Babies under

1 year old need less than 1g of salt per day, which they usually get from breast milk or formula. Salty foods such as store-bought sausage, bacon, and chips should not be included in their daily diet.

Sugar

Adding sugary products to a baby's diet can lead to the development of a sweet palate, tooth decay, and child obesity. This doesn't apply to the natural sugars present in fruits, vegetables, and milk. You can add fruits instead of sugar to their meals to sweeten them.

Artificial food colorants

I know how hard it is to say "No" to colorful food. The brighter the color, the more loudly it says, "Eat Me." Artificial food colorants are next on the avoid list, because some research indicates that AFCs might impact the behavior of a small number of kids, possibly resulting in hyperactivity or attention-deficit/hyperactivity disorder (ADHD). Other research has shown that AFCs may increase hyperactivity without resulting in behavior associated with ADHD. Therefore, avoiding products that contain AFCs would be a good decision.

Furthermore, you can incorporate natural food colors from different vegetables and fruits into your kid's food. Below are some examples of fruits and veggies with great natural color.

- Pink: strawberries, raspberries
- Red: beetroot, tomato
- Orange: carrots, paprika, saffron, orange sweet potato
- Yellow: saffron powder, turmeric
- Green: matcha, spinach
- Blue: red cabbage + baking soda
- Purple: blueberries, blackberries, purple sweet potato

Runny egg

The USDA states that soft-boiled/sunny-side-up eggs with runny yolks are not safe for babies to consume. According to the Centers for Disease Control and Prevention (CDC), kids under the age of 5 have higher rates of salmonella than any other age group. Salmonella is the type of bacteria that's the most frequently reported cause of food-related illness in the United States. It can cause an upset stomach, diarrhea, fever, pain, and cramping in the baby's belly.

Raw shellfish and high-mercury-level fish

Undercooked shellfish such as shrimp, oysters, lobster, and crab should be completely avoided as it can cause food poisoning. You can introduce well-cooked shellfish when your baby is 9 to 10 months old.

Fish with high mercury levels, such as swordfish and marlin, should be avoided as they can affect a baby's developing nervous system. Offer oily fish instead: tuna, salmon, or mackerel.

Cow's milk

Cow's milk must be avoided as the main drink until your baby is 1 year old as it lacks the right balance of nutrients for infants. Nevertheless, small amounts of cow's milk can be added to a baby's cooked meal or cereals from 6 months onwards. As previously mentioned, try to use full-fat dairy products.

Whole nuts

Don't serve whole nuts to your baby until he is 5 years old because whole nuts can present a choking hazard and nuts such as peanuts, walnuts, and hazelnuts are potentially allergenic foods. Nuts that have been ground or smooth nut butter can be given from 6-7 months onwards. If there is a history of allergy in your family, check with your pediatrician before introducing potential allergens to your baby.

Coffee and tea

Caffeine not only disrupts a baby's sleep but also reduces iron absorption, which can be detrimental to a baby's health and can increase the risk of anemia. Offer sips of water with meals instead.

Allergenic foods

Starting semi-solids can be a thrilling milestone for you, even though it comes with some concerns and questions, typically about food allergies. What foods can cause allergies to your baby? How can we avoid them?

Emerging research has shown that delaying the introduction of allergenic foods to the baby doesn't reduce the risk of having allergies in the future. The American Academy of Pediatrics (AAP) says that allergenic foods can be introduced to children at the same time as other foods, around 4 to 6 months, which might reduce the chances of having a severe allergic reaction. Research suggests it could lower the chance of developing the allergy altogether. It also suggests that all babies should be introduced to peanuts during their first year of life, regardless of food allergy risk.

Still, it's a good idea to check in with your pediatrician before introducing allergenic foods to your little one.

Up to the present time, there are more than 100 allergenic foods, but certain foods are more allergenic than others. Below are 8 foods that are known to cause allergic reactions in some people.

Foundation

The Top 8 Allergenic Foods

- Peanuts
- Cow's milk
- Eggs
- Tree nuts (such as walnuts or almonds)
- Fish
- Shellfish
- Soy
- Food contains gluten, such as wheat and barley

If there is no history of allergic disease (atopy), including eczema, asthma, and hayfever, in your family, the risk of a serious reaction is low. On the other hand, having a history of food allergies in the family can double the chances of your baby developing one. Though it's not inevitable, the chances are still high at 50-50. However, the best way to take the lead with allergenic foods is to introduce all 8 allergens individually and gradually in small amounts at an interval of 1 to 2 weeks. This way, you can identify any allergies that might develop.

> What is allergic reaction? When the body's immune system gets confused and reacts to proteins in food, it releases the chemical histamine, which may cause skin rashes, swelling, vomiting or diarrhea.

Yet again, I would remind you to check in with your pediatrician before introducing allergens to your little one because allergic reactions can lead to anaphylaxis or anaphylactic shock. Keep an eye out for the following symptoms and immediately contact your pediatrician if your child reacts.

Foods to avoid and allergenic foods

- Hives or welts
- Flushed skin or rash
- Face, tongue, or lip swelling
- Vomiting and/or diarrhea

- Coughing or wheezing
- Difficulty breathing
- Loss of consciousness

The positive news is that, for the most part, children outgrow some allergies, such as egg and milk, at the age of 5, but some allergies last longer than normal and infrequently aren't outgrown, such as allergies to fish, nuts, and shellfish.

Plot and plan

There is an architectural term "plot and plan" which refers to having a plot and then designing a plan until it is a complete building. Similarly, your baby is a plot, and you frame your baby into a healthy eater, regardless of which method you choose to wean your baby.

Traditional spoon feeding vs baby-led weaning

No matter how exciting it is to wean the baby, we often get stuck on either spoon-feeding or baby-led weaning. Let me briefly explain what these methods are, and then you can decide which works best for you.

Traditional spoon-feeding

This is a traditional method of feeding puréed food to your baby. The baby learns to eat blended food, then progresses to mashed foods and then chopped foods. Traditional spoon-feeding (TSF) is a great switch from milk to baby food and then to table food. This method is less likely to create gagging incidents as foods are more controllable by parents. However, babies who are on TSF are less likely to

sit with families during mealtimes, or one of the parents has to feed the baby during the meal. This method is less messy, so you will get to know how much your baby has eaten. Sometimes, it is hard for the baby to accept other textures if he gets used to smooth textures.

Baby-led weaning

Baby-led weaning (BLW) is a practice in which the baby learns to self-feed by being in charge of the food. Items such as fruit, cooked vegetables, meat, and cheese are cut into suitably sized slices that infants can hold. In BLW, the baby goes directly to solid foods, rather than starting with puréed or mashed foods. This method of giving finger foods has been widely propagated in the past few decades.

BLW is an admirable method in which the baby works on his oral skills and fine motor skills. Another plus is that you can eat together as the baby feeds himself, but, initially, you must embrace oodles of food being thrown onto the table and floor during mealtimes. You may feel as though you're wasting lots of food while your baby is learning to taste new flavors and a variety of food.

Besides choosing any one method, traditional or BLW, you can opt to go with both methods. You offer purées along with finger foods.

Puréed foods can be fed by you, whereas baby practices BLW with other food that is easy to eat and cut into fingers. The choice is yours.

Regardless of what method you choose, remember we are new parents and we're still learning. Take it slow and embrace the mess created by your baby. Make it fun, and don't get stressed over mealtime if your baby doesn't eat much. They say, "Food is just for fun before one." And a quick reminder, milk is a major source of nutrients for the baby until one.

Preterm weaning

Weaning preterm babies is more complicated. Because they're premature, their digestive system isn't fully established. Consequently, they find it difficult to suck and swallow the food correctly. It is advised that preterm babies should be introduced to solid foods between 5 and 8 months of chronological age, provided they have reached at least three months of corrected age. Preterm babies have an additional need for certain nutrients such as iron and zinc. Ensure you provide nutrition-rich foods, for instance, avocado and lentils, and consult your pediatrician before weaning.

> Babies born before 37 weeks are judged as preterm.

Choking and gagging in babies

Moms often worry about choking in babies if they're served finger foods. I did, too, when I started BLW. Well, here comes an interesting fact which I didn't know: the risk of choking isn't eliminated by any weaning method. A small survey by various pediatricians noticed no significant difference in choking incidents between TSF and BLW infants. Nevertheless, BLW has a low choking risk in comparison to TSF because babies at six months of age already have the ability to chew. They can chew and swallow their foods even if their teeth are not yet present. They know how to manipulate the food in their mouth. TSF babies, on the other hand, rarely get finger foods, tend to hold food in their mouths, and think they do not need to exercise their jaws to chew. This presents the risk of choking.

Every parent/caregiver must distinguish between choking and gagging.

Choking:

A complete blockage of the airway caused by food or any other substance is called choking. A baby who is choking will not be able to breathe or make sounds as air cannot pass through his airways. The baby will be in discomfort, will try to grab his throat, and might turn to blue.

This requires intervention by an adult to force the food from the airway and mouth. Hold the child face down over your arm, with the head slightly lower than the chest. Give 5 quick and powerful blows between the child's shoulder blades with the palm of your free hand. (If nothing works, see the doctor immediately.)

Choking is more dangerous if it occurs before 12 months of age.

Thus, to prevent choking hazard avoid foods such as popcorn, raw carrot chunks, whole dried fruit, and whole grapes. Cut grapes and berries in half, and remove any pips before you dish them up to your baby. You must be around the baby while they're eating – it's better to be safe than sorry.

Furthermore, I would strongly suggest you watch videos of choking relief for infants before starting solids.

Gagging/Gag reflex:

The gag reflex is a sensitive mechanism to protect babies from swallowing pieces of food that are too large. Gagging protects them from choking hazards and is quite common in BLW babies because it is provoked by stimuli closer to the front of the mouth and farther away from the airway. Sooner or later, BLW babies learn to keep large pieces of food away from their airways.

Gagging is a typical reflex that can arise when babies reach six months of age. Gagging is also common in babies who are learning to self-feed. Gagging happens when foods move to the back of the mouth, and babies cough and splutter then bring the food back to the front of their mouth again. Unlike choking, gagging is usually noisy, and because of gagging incidents, most moms end up choosing TSP so they can control the foods they feed to their baby.

Eating environment

Zia was never interested in having meals alone. I sensed he always wanted to enjoy and be a part of our mealtimes. When I started baby-led weaning, I made sure to have at least one meal of the day with him initially. He left me to ponder how these little humans learn from us. How they try to imitate our actions, eating style, and behavior while having meals. I bet you they see it all, not just what they're eating but also what their family is eating.

There's plenty of research saying that kids who eat with their families actually do better in terms of their emotional well-being. Eating together is an opportunity to pass on family traditions. Kids and adults record their memories and pass those on. You can also call a few of your friends to have dinner at your place and involve your babies and kids to show how meals are also involved in social communication.

Switch off the television, avoid using gadgets, and try to create a calm atmosphere. If your child has already started to be weaned, some nice baby music may uplift your baby's mood. No wonder some babies eat well with a little bit of distraction. A spoon or a washable toy might entertain him while you slide the spoon into his mouth. Always make your baby sit in a highchair before serving food so that he can anticipate what is going to happen. A plastic mat or cloth spread under the highchair may help for cleaning up and recycling food, and lots of patience is required.

Eating out

Being a social butterfly, I love meeting people and dining out. Likewise, I suspect Zia has another level of energy when he goes out and finds children around him. I believe dining out is a great way to encourage flexibility in children. They learn to share meals, socialize, and communicate. Yet dining out with a toddler is no piece of cake; it demands lots of patience and planning for your little one.

Dropping some tips for consideration:

- It's good if you feed your kid before leaving home so when you arrive, he won't be hungry. You can offer him the snacks you packed for him, or you can order some snacks in the restaurant.

Plot and plan

- Taking a tired toddler out is a big NO. Plan according to his nap/sleep schedules. After all, it's a matter of your child's needs. Or do you want your child to create a complete disaster at the restaurant?
- Make sure you have enough supplies to entertain him because toddlers find it difficult to sit still in a highchair. A quick walk might work to press the restart button and refresh him so he will be willing to sit again.
- Pack his favorite food or something dry so that he can munch without getting nasty. You can take a suction bowl and baby-friendly cutlery as most restaurants don't provide them, and a suction bowl will prevent food from falling.
- Always be prepared to leave. Sometimes kids react differently when their environment changes and plans don't always work out, so be ready to leave if things get ugly.

Healthy snacking

Have you ever wondered why kids get hungry 30 minutes after eating a bag of chips or candy bars?

It is something called the "glycemic index" (GI). It's a value designated to foods based on how slowly or rapidly they increase blood sugar

(glucose) levels. Foods comprised of refined, processed carbs and longer cooking times break down into glucose more quickly; hence, they have a higher GI. The faster the sugar level rises, the more quickly it drops, and kids are soon hungry again.

Foods that contain fiber, protein, and fats release glucose more slowly; therefore, they have a lower GI. Kids won't get hungry quickly if you serve them food or snacks which have a lower or medium GI that is more filling. Ensure there is a good balance of nutrients so the snacks are sustaining; they will slow down the release of sugar into the blood and add to the quality of the kid's diet. I'm sure there are plenty of foods in your pantry that contain fiber and protein. For example, apple slices and cheddar cheese, hummus and vegetable sticks, a bowl of fruit salad, and peanut butter and crackers.

> Young kids can have 2 to 3 healthy snacks every day.

> Snacks are to be served a few hours before or after a meal.

Remember, small tummies need small servings, and kids who spend a lot of their time munching have a hard time during meals. Putting a halt to snacking just before meals may promote more healthy, appetizing mealtimes for kids.

*See page 225 for snack ideas.

Dealing with fussy eaters

Picky eaters are quite common. Most kids become fussy eaters to some extent, though I would rather say that picky eating is a normal development stage for toddlers. After completing one year, a toddler's appetite tends to slow down. I remember thinking my son was a fussy eater because he didn't eat for 3 weeks. Do you know why? Because I wasn't serving food at the same time every day as per our routine. I was busy and didn't look after him well when he was hungry. Subsequently, he started eating when I reestablished our routine and served him at same time every day in his highchair.

There can be reasons behind picky eating, yet many toddlers outgrow their eating behavior with perseverance and proper guidance towards nutritious eating. I'm presenting a few suggestions that might help you.

Model healthy eating

According to USDA, kids between the ages of 12 months and 24 months are most likely to adopt their eating habits from their surroundings, such as parents, elder siblings, or other people at home. It is imperative to model healthy eating habits around your kids as they like to imitate and follow you. So, next time if you want your toddler to eat broccoli, you got to eat it too!

Eating environment

The home environment is one of the determining factors shaping your child's upbringing. Kids who practiced eating healthy food together at home are anticipated to persist in positive eating habits in the future.

Endeavor to have one meal together as a family every day. Escape from television and gadgets during mealtimes; these are distractions. Instead, have positive conversations and try to avoid arguments and debates during mealtimes.

Involvement in the meal preparation

Involving kids in meal planning puts them in charge of something they look forward to, offers them two-three healthy options, and lets them pick what they want to eat. Letting them help you to prepare their meal in the kitchen needs a lot of supervision.

Therefore, start with baby steps such as pouring and mixing. If your kids are 4 years or older, kids' cutlery can be used to cut veggies.

Let your children pluck herbs from the kitchen garden or choose fruits/veggies from the farmers' market for dinner. Having a kitchen garden at home plays a vital role, and getting kids involved in the garden can encourage them to eat fruits and vegetables.

Make food fun

Kids love colorful things, so why not making boring food fun by adding a pop of color or giving it a shape or the face of an animal. This will fascinate kids and entice them to try the food.

Try and try again

Kids sometimes refuse to eat, but that doesn't mean we should stop trying. It takes a couple of times before a child's taste buds accept something new. Keep presenting a variety of new foods as well as those they didn't like before. Also remember, occasionally kids don't feel well. Maybe because of teething, a mild fever, sleep regression, etc., they don't feel like eating anything at all. Just keep trying!

Avoid food fights and treats

Avoid enforcing and punishing during meals. If your child refuses to eat, that can lead to consequences such as actively disliking the food, which may be liked without the pressure. Bribing may be tempting yet presenting treats for finishing a meal will lead to future fights.

Routine

Kids are keen to follow the routine. Schedule their meals and eat at the same time every day so their minds can anticipate when it is time to eat.

Division of Responsibilities

The Satter Division of Responsibilities in feeding is an another griming perspective to combat pressure and picky eating habits. The phenomena proposed that parents are to choose WHAT, WHEN and WHERE of feeding and the child chooses "how much" and "whether to eat" of what ever you choose to feed.

These habits can be established from infancy such as you chose to give "formula" or "breastmilk" and let your infant ask for the milk, let him decide how much and how often he wants. Hence, encouraging whether to eat, the quantity, to enjoy the food and to be well-behaved at the family mealtime. Your responsibility is to make structured family meals and snack time. Make sure it should be pleasant, enjoyable and without pressure because it has tremendous effects on child mental and physical health.

How to cut food for baby-led weaning

So why do we call finger food? Because food is long enough for baby to hold in his fist and half of it pops out the top of his fist for him to munch on. Foods are cut into finger strips where possible, roughly 2.5 to 3 in (7.5cm) long and ½ in (2cm) wide. Just like an adult finger! Liquid food such as soup and yogurt can be spoonfed or you can use two spoons, one for you and one for your baby to help himself. It gets a lot nastier than you think, but then again, the more you allow your baby to use a spoon the more quickly he will learn to feed himself.

Dropping some examples for you as a guide:

- **Boiled egg quarters – cut lengthwise**

- **Cooked meat/chicken – boneless, cut into small strips.**

- **Kiwi fruit – peeled and cut into rounds or wedges lengthwise.**

- **Cucumber/carrot – finger strips**

- **Grapes/berries – cut in half or quarters, lengthwise.**

- **Pancakes/patties – cut into strips**

- **Oranges – cut into wedges, lengthwise; remove membrane, and remove any seeds.**

- **Peas/sweetcorn – served whole (too small to choke on).**

Equipment/tools needed

There are a few things that are nice to have before you start feeding semi-solids to your little one.

Blender: If you have opted for the traditional feeding method, it's a help to invest in a good blender to make large batches for freezing. An electric hand blender is another option to blend small quantities of baby food/purée.

Steamer (optional): Steaming food is a great method to preserve nutrients, rather than boiling food. A steam basket is a less expensive choice.

Highchair: Make sure your baby is safely and securely seated while you feed him and never leave him unattended when he is eating.

Large plastic mat: A mat under the highchair makes it easy to recycle food and clean up afterward.

Bib/long-sleeved bib/catcher These will prevent baby's clothes from getting dirty.

Suction bowl/plate: For me, this is a must-have because most babies try to flip or throw their plate from the tray and food ends up on the floor.

Cup and baby-friendly cutlery: An open cup or straw cup for water during mealtimes and cutlery such as a silicone spoon that isn't hard on baby's gums. As he improves, you can also let your baby eat with baby-friendly cutlery.

Ice cube tray: Purée can be frozen in an ice-cube tray during the first few weeks.

Storage containers: A good selection is helpful for storing and freezing baby food.

Cooking terms

When I began BLW, a few terms were tricky to understand. I remember Googling words every time I made any BLW food for my son. You might be a first-time mom or a cooking expert, but let's have a look at some cooking terms before we start on the recipes.

Slice, Chop, Dice

Slice: to cut large ingredients/items into similar flat shapes or pieces. For example, tomato slices, onion rings, carrot coins.

Chop: to cut into smaller, roughly squarish pieces between ½ inch to ¾ inch. Herbs such as coriander or mint can be roughly or finely chopped.

Dice: to chop into cubes varying in size between ½ inch and ¼ inch. The motive is to make food look attractive and tempting. For example, diced mango.

Julienne, Shred, Grate

Julienne: to cut long, thin, matchstick-like pieces. For example, julienned carrots.

Shred: to cut much smaller strips than julienne. This can be achieved using a coarse hand grater or box grater. For example, shredded carrot, shredded zucchini.

Grate: to use a grater to cut food into the smallest pieces. For example, grated garlic, grated cheese.

Pinch, seasoning to taste

Pinch: approximately $\frac{1}{16}$ of a teaspoon.

Seasoning to taste: any spices that appeal to your taste, in the quantities you prefer.

Mince, Mash, Purée

Mince: using a mincer to cut food into the tiniest pieces. It doesn't need to be uniform. For example, chicken mince or minced garlic.

Mash: using a fork or your hand to smash the food into a pulp that may contain lumps. For example, mashed banana or mashed potato.

Purée: to blend food to a smooth consistency. A food processor or blender is used to achieve a purée. For, example, sweet potato purée, tomato purée.

Roast, Bake, Grill

Roast: Food is cooked in the oven at a high temperature for a longer period. For example, a whole chicken is roasted in the oven.

Bake: Food is cooked in the oven at a lower temperature without coming into contact with the flame. Bread and desserts are usually baked.

Grill: Food is placed on a heated grill rack or over the flame for a short period. It doesn't require an oven. Certain meats and vegetables can be grilled.

Sauté, Deep fry, Shallow fry

Sauté: to fry food on high heat for a short period with a little oil/fat. For example, sautéed mushrooms.

Deep Fry: to submerge food in hot oil. You may need a deep pan to accommodate enough oil for deep frying. For example, crispy chicken and French fries are to be deep fried. They cook from all sides and get a crispy coating.

Shallow Fry: to cook food with less oil. Shallow or pan-frying is used for delicate foods that may fall a part in deep frying, for example, fritters and pancakes.

Boil, Simmer, Steam

Boil: to cook food in liquid at a high temperature (approximately 212 degrees). Bubbles rise audibly to the surface. This method is commonly used for pasta.

Simmer: a more gentle method in which the liquid stays below boiling point. Tiny bubbles may appear.

Steam: to cook food in a steamer bucket placed over boiling water. Steamed food doesn't lose its nutrients or flavor. For example, steamed vegetables.

Knead, Whisk, Whip

Knead: to massage or work with the hands to make a dough, for example, for a loaf of bread.

Whisk: to stir quickly with a help of a fork or a whisk.

Whip: to beat an ingredient energetically to incorporate air till it becomes a foamy cream. For example, cream or egg whites. You can use a beater for whipping.

Marinate, Steep

Marinate: to soak meat, for example, in a seasoned liquid for a particular time before cooking. It helps to enhance the flavor of the dish.

Cooking terms

Steep: to soak ingredients or spices in water or other liquid to extract the flavor. For example, a teabag in a cup of hot water.

Glaze, Zest

Glaze: a glossy coating, such as melted chocolate, poured over a portion of food.

Zest: the grated outer skin of citrus fruit such as orange, lemon, and lime. The colored part of the skin contains natural oils which provide aroma and flavor.

The ingredients your kitchen needs

80% of the items on this list have a long shelf life, so I always try to stock these items in my pantry. If you have a few things from this list, you can make healthy and tasty food for your little ones without rushing to the grocery store.

Flours & grains

- Wheat flour
- All-purpose flour
- Pancake mix
- Corn flour (cornstarch)
- Rolled or instant oats
- Whole-grain cereals
- Rice Krispies
- Lentils
- Beans
- Long-grained white rice
- Brown rice
- Chickpeas
- Chickpea/gram flour
- Regular and whole-grain pasta

The ingredients your kitchen needs

Dairy

- Full-fat cow's milk
- Yogurt
- Cheddar cheese
- Cheddar cheese sticks
- Unsalted butter
- Full-fat cream
- Cream cheese

Frozen foods

- Frozen mixed vegetables
- Frozen broccoli
- Frozen prawns

Fruits & vegetables

- Apples
- Bananas
- Kiwifruit
- Strawberries
- Blackberries
- Raspberries
- Blueberries
- Lemons
- Spinach
- Onions
- Garlic bulbs
- Ginger
- Potatoes
- Capsicums
- Cucumbers
- Carrots

Condiments/spices & baking aids

- Salt
- Black and white pepper
- Paprika
- Garam masala
- Cumin (whole/ground)
- Turmeric
- Low-salt vegetable and chicken stock cubes
- Sunflower oil
- Olive oil
- Ketchup
- Vinegar
- Chia seeds
- Desiccated coconut
- Low-salt soy sauce
- Ginger garlic paste
- Smooth peanut butter
- Baking powder
- Baking soda
- Sugar
- Vanilla extract
- Honey
- Maple syrup
- Sprinkles
- Ready-to-roll puff pastry

Poultry & meat

- Eggs
- Chicken
- Fish
- Mutton

Basic cooking measurement conversions

Dry/Weight

Teaspoon	Tablespoon	Cups	Ounces	Grams
1 teaspoon	1/3 tablespoon		1/6 ounce	
3 teaspoons	1 tablespoon		1/2 ounce	14 grams
6 teaspoons	2 tablespoons	1/8 cup	1 ounce	28 grams
12 teaspoons	4 tablespoons	1/4 cup	2 ounces	56.7 grams
	8 tablespoons	1/2 cup	4 ounces	113 grams
	16 tablespoons	1 cup	8 ounces	225 grams

Liquid or Volume

Teaspoon	Tablespoon	Cups	Fluid ounce	ml
1 teaspoon	1/3 tablespoon		1/6 fl. ounce	5ml
3 teaspoons	1 tablespoon		1/2 fl. ounce	15ml
6 teaspoons	2 tablespoons	1/8 cup	1 fl. ounce	29.5ml
12 teaspoons	4 tablespoons	1/4 cup	2 fl. ounces	59ml
	8 tablespoons	1/2 cup	4 fl. ounces	118ml
	16 tablespoons	1 cup	8 fl. ounces	237ml

Storing and thawing baby food

Baby food is as delicate as the baby because wrongly stored baby food can generate bacteria and endanger the baby's life. It is most important to follow the guidelines so that you can avoid your baby's food becoming contaminated. The recommendations below are adopted from USDA Home-Prepared Infant Food guidelines.

- Always wash your hands before preparing and storing baby food.
- Puréed baby food should not be kept for more than 2 hours at room temperature.
- If planning to refrigerate or freeze puréed food, place it straight into the refrigerator after processing or freeze it immediately. (If hot, let it cool at room temperature and then freeze.)

- Keep it in an air-tight container and don't forget to label it with a date. Food can be stored for up to 2 days in the refrigerator for 1 to 2 months in the freezer. (Meats and eggs must be consumed within 24 hours).
- Always cover the baby food. Open food becomes a breeding ground for bacteria.
- Defrosted puréed food cannot be refrozen; however, food prepared from frozen fruits/veggies can be refrozen.

For freezing, there are two methods:

- Ice cube tray method: Pour cooled, puréed baby food into the cavities of a clean ice cube tray and cover with foil. When frozen solid, store cubes in the freezer in a freezer bag, Ziplock bag, or airtight box.
- Cookie sheet method: Drop little heaps of 1-2 tablespoons of puréed food onto a cookie sheet, then cover with plastic wrap or foil and freeze. Once frozen, place the drops of frozen puréed baby food in an airtight container and return to the freezer.

Thawing and warming

- Baby food should not be thawed at room temperature due to contamination. However, it can be thawed in the refrigerator overnight or under running lukewarm water.
- Thawed baby food cannot be frozen again, and leftovers should be consumed within 2 hours or thrown away.

Storing and thawing baby food

- Frozen cubes can be reheated in a heat-resistant container in a pan of hot water.
- To microwave, you must use a microwave-safe dish. After heating, stir the puréed baby food to avoid hot spots. Baby food should feel lukewarm and be tested before feeding.

Structure

LEVEL 1 – From 6 months to 7 months

First foods

As mentioned in part 1, the ideal age for weaning is 6 months since a baby's digestive system is mature enough to digest blended foods and finger foods carefully introduced alongside purées. Keep in mind that your baby's milk intake must not be reduced as milk is still the key source of nutrients for the growth and development of your baby. Don't anticipate that your baby will eat more than one or two tablespoons in his first few weeks. Don't be too hasty; schedule one mealtime first when you are both relaxed and comfortable.

Many parents choose to start with rice cereals as their first baby food. I prefer to introduce nutritious fruit and vegetable purées from the beginning. In the first few weeks, baby should ingest single-ingredient purées that are easy to digest. This also makes it easier to avoid allergic reactions. Appropriate fruits and veggies ought to be processed or cooked before feeding to your baby and offered for 2 or 3 days in succession to acclimatize your baby's taste buds. Good luck, mummy!

Below are some single-ingredient purée recipes:

Carrot

2 to 3 medium-sized carrots peeled and evenly chopped. Boil the water in a saucepan, add the steamer basket loaded with carrot chunks, and cover.

Steam until tender, which will take 15 to 20 minutes, depending on the thickness of the chunks. Put the carrot chunks in a blender and blend until smooth. Add breast milk/formula or a dash of water to achieve a smooth consistency.

> **POINT TO BE NOTED!**
> Steaming is preferable to boiling since steamed veggies/fruits preserve more nutrients as they remain out of the boiling water.

Serve in a bowl, or store in the freezer for 1-2 months. (For storing baby food, see page 37.)

Sweet potato

One large sweet potato, peeled and cubed. Boil the water in a saucepan, add the steamer basket loaded with sweet potato chunks, and cover.

Steam until tender (15 to 20 minutes), then blend until smooth. Add water or breastmilk/formula if required. Serve or store for later.

Parsnip

2 medium-sized parsnips peeled and evenly chopped. Boil the water in a saucepan, add the steamer basket loaded with parsnip chunks, and cover.

Steam until tender, which will take 15 to 20 minutes, depending on the thickness of the chunks. Put the parsnip chunks in a blender and blend until smooth. Add breast milk/formula or a dash of water to achieve a smooth consistency.

Serve in a bowl, or store in the freezer for 1-2 months. (For storing baby food, see page 37.)

Peas

1 to 2 cups of peas, shelled. Bring a little water to a boil in a saucepan, add the peas to a steamer basket, and cover. If using fresh peas, steam for 10 to 15 minutes until tender. (Frozen peas will take about 5 minutes.) Reserve the water.

Purée until smooth. Add breast/formula or remaining boiled water if needed to thin.

Swede

2 to 3 swedes, scrubbed or peeled and cubed. Boil the water in a saucepan, add the steamer basket loaded with swede chunks, and cover.

Steam until tender, which will take 15 to 20 minutes, depending on the thickness of the chunks.

Put the swede chunks in a blender and blend until smooth. Add breast milk/formula or a dash of water to achieve a smooth consistency.

Serve in a bowl, or store in the freezer for 1-2 months. (For storing baby food, see page 37.)

Papaya

Cut a ripe papaya in half and remove all the black seeds. Peel it and cut it into chunks.

Transfer to a blender or food processor and blend until smooth.

Serve or freeze for up to 2 months.

Mango

3 medium-sized ripe mangoes, skinned and stoned. (No need to cook.)

Purée the pulp, serve or freeze for later!!

Peach

3 to 4 skinned and stoned peaches.

Blend the peaches if they are ripe; otherwise, steam them first for 5 minutes until tender.

Serve or freeze.

Banana

Mashed banana is ideal baby food. It's easy to digest, a good source of fiber, vitamin B6, and Vitamin C, and unlikely to prompt an allergy.

Mash 1 peeled, ripe banana with the back of a fork until smooth. Add breastmilk/formula or boiled water to reach the desired consistency.

Apple

2 sweet apples peeled, cored, and diced.

Transfer the apple chunks to a saucepan, bring to the boil in a little water, cover, and simmer for about 15 minutes.

You can add a pinch of cinnamon powder or a small stick of cinnamon. (Remove it before blending.)

Blend in a food processor to an even texture. Serve, or double the batch for freezing.

Blackberries

Put a handful of blackberries in a blender and purée until smooth. (No need to cook.)

Serve directly or store in the refrigerator for up to 24 hours.

Rice cereal

There are hundreds of rice cereals out there with added salt, sugar, and preservatives. This recipe is easy to make and loaded with nutrients.

Pour 2 to 3 cups of water into a saucepan and boil.

Add 1 cup ground rice, 1 tbsp oil, and ¼ tsp ground cardamom and stir until the desired consistency is reached. Add breast milk/formula if needed.

Semolina (soji) cereal

Dry roast ½ cup semolina until golden. Pour 2 to 3 cups of water into a saucepan and bring it to a boil.

Add roasted semolina, a knob of butter, and ¼ teaspoon cardamom, let it absorb the water, and transfer to a bowl. Add breast/formula or cow's milk to reach the desired consistency. Purée in a blender if a creamy smooth texture is desired.

Sabu dana/sago/tapioca pearl cereal

Sabu dana is good for gaining weight and giving babies instant energy, especially when they are sick and have diarrhea. Try offering it once in a while since it has no important nutrients.

Soak ¼ cup of Sabu dana for 1 hour and drain the water. Transfer it to a saucepan, and add 1 cup of water. Cook on low heat until it becomes translucent.

Add ¼ teaspoon jaggery, 1 tablespoon butter, and ¼ teaspoon cardamom and mix well. Add ½ cup milk and let it simmer for 5 minutes on low heat. Remove from stove once milk gets thick.

Cow/breast milk or formula can be added if cereal gets very thick.

6 months to 7 months

Schematic Weekly Planner

week 1

	DAY 1	DAY 2	DAY 3	DAY 4	DAY 5	DAY 6	DAY 7
EARLY MORNING	Breast/formula milk	Breast/formula milk	Breast/formula milk	Breast/formula milk	Breast/formula milk	Breast/formula milk	Breast/formula milk
BREAKFAST	Sweet potato	Sweet potato	Sweet potato	Apple	Apple	Apple	Carrot
LUNCH	Breast/formula milk	Breast/formula milk	Breast/formula milk	Breast/formula milk	Breast/formula milk	Breast/formula milk	Breast/formula milk
SNACKS	Breast/formula milk	Breast/formula milk	Breast/formula milk	Breast/formula milk	Breast/formula milk	Breast/formula milk	Breast/formula milk
DINNER	Breast/formula milk	Breast/formula milk	Breast/formula milk	Breast/formula milk	Breast/formula milk	Breast/formula milk	Breast/formula milk

week 2

	DAY 1	DAY 2	DAY 3	DAY 4	DAY 5	DAY 6	DAY 7
EARLY MORNING	Breast/formula milk	Breast/formula milk	Breast/formula milk	Breast/formula milk	Breast/formula milk	Breast/formula milk	Breast/formula milk
BREAKFAST	Carrot	Rice cereal	Rice cereal	Peas	Peas	Parsnip	Parsnip
LUNCH	Breast/formula milk	Breast/formula milk	Breast/formula milk	Breast/formula milk	Breast/formula milk	Breast/formula milk	Breast/formula milk
SNACKS	Breast/formula milk	Breast/formula milk	Breast/formula milk	Breast/formula milk	Breast/formula milk	Breast/formula milk	Breast/formula milk
DINNER	Breast/formula milk	Breast/formula milk	Breast/formula milk	Breast/formula milk	Breast/formula milk	Breast/formula milk	Breast/formula milk

week 3

	DAY 1	DAY 2	DAY 3	DAY 4	DAY 5	DAY 6	DAY 7
EARLY MORNING	Breast/formula milk	Breast/formula milk	Breast/formula milk	Breast/formula milk	Breast/formula milk	Breast/formula milk	Breast/formula milk
BREAKFAST	Peach	Semolina cereal	Banana	Peas	Swede	Mango or papaya	Sweet potato
LUNCH	Breast/formula milk	Breast/formula milk	Breast/formula milk	Breast/formula milk	Breast/formula milk	Breast/formula milk	Breast/formula milk
SNACKS	Breast/formula milk	Breast/formula milk	Breast/formula milk	Breast/formula milk	Breast/formula milk	Breast/formula milk	Breast/formula milk
DINNER	Breast/formula milk	Breast/formula milk	Breast/formula milk	Breast/formula milk	Breast/formula milk	Breast/formula milk	Breast/formula milk

*Maintain the usual milk intake during the night.

LEVEL 2 – From 7 months to 9 months

First foods to finger foods

Your baby's hand grasp is developing and he can hold finger foods properly, manipulate food in his mouth, and swallow it more efficiently.

After the acceptance of first foods or single-ingredient purées, you can serve him multiple-ingredient purées and encourage finger foods.

While offering puréed food, use two spoons, one for you to feed him and one for the baby to feed himself. Remember, the more he practices, the sooner he will learn to feed himself.

Now, this can be a lot messier than you thought. Having a suction bowl and large plastic mat under the highchair could be a good idea if your baby attempts to play with the food or tosses the bowl. Aim to have one meal together with your little one when you both are relaxed and fresh. Constantly model how to eat the food you are serving to the baby and make sure your little one isn't tired; otherwise, he might not be interested in eating. I know it is hard to take when your baby doesn't eat and plays with his food, but then again, letting your baby play with food is also a kind of sensory play, so try not to panic and embrace the mess. Nevertheless, give the baby his usual milk in between mealtimes since it is the major source of nutrients for babies under 12 months.

Purées

Apple Peaches Apricot Purée  TIME: 20 MINS

This blend, containing carbs, vitamin C, fiber, and a hint of iron is great for energy. Serve it as a purée or make healthy ice lollies for your teething baby.

MATERIAL

- 1 large apple peeled, cored, and diced
- 2 peaches, peeled and pitted
- 4 to 5 dried apricots
- Pinch of turmeric
- Pinch of ground cinnamon
- 1 tbsp basil seeds (soaked)

CONSTRUCTION

Put apple chunks in a saucepan and boil in a little water for about 10 minutes. Cover and cook on low heat until tender.

Transfer apple chunks to a blender, together with peaches and dried apricots. Purée until smooth.

Add the cinnamon, turmeric, and basil seeds. Stir well. (Add breastmilk/formula/coconut milk for a smoother texture.)

Broccoli Potato Blend

 TIME: 15 MINS

Loaded with carbs, essential vitamins and minerals that makes it an ideal nutritional blend for babies.

MATERIAL

- 1 big potato, peeled and diced
- 1 cup broccoli, broken into small florets

CONSTRUCTION

Either steam vegetables in a steam basket or place in a saucepan and simmer in a little water for 10 minutes until tender but florets still green in color.

Transfer potato and florets to a bowl and mash with a fork or blend in a food processor or with a blender until smooth. Serve or freeze.

Dragon Fruit and Peach

 **TIME: 10 MINS**

This puree is full of fiber, vitamin C, magnesium, antioxidants and a little bit of iron great for your little one's immune system.

MATERIAL

- 1 dragon fruit cut into chunks
- 2 ripe peaches, peeled and pitted

CONSTRUCTION

Blend or hand mash dragon fruit chunks and peaches. Mix well and serve or freeze for later.

Pea and Sweet Potato

 TIME: 15 MINS

This healthy blend contains a bit of everything and is good for your little one's growth and digestive system.

MATERIAL

- ½ cup shelled peas and green beans (fresh or frozen)
- 1 medium-sized orange sweet potato, peeled and finely chopped
- Pinch of ground cumin
- ½ cup quinoa, rinsed (optional)

CONSTRUCTION

Put quinoa in a saucepan and add 2 cups of water. Bring it to a boil over high heat. When only a little water is left, remove the pan from the heat and set it aside with the lid on to steam for 5 to 10 minutes.

Steam the sweet potato, green beans, and peas transfer to a deep bowl, add the fluffy quinoa and ground cumin and give it a good stir.

After mixing, mash with a fork or masher. Your textured purée is ready to serve!

Peach Chia Pudding

 TIME: 10 MINS

Add texture to a regular purée by adding nutritious chia seeds. Chia seeds contain fiber, omega-3 fatty acids, protein, and several essential minerals.

MATERIAL

- 3 to 4 ripe peaches, peeled and pitted
- 2 tbsp chia seeds, soaked

CONSTRUCTION

Place peach slices in a blender and blend until smooth.

Add soaked chia seeds for extra texture. Add water, breastmilk, or formula as needed to thin. If too runny, add baby rice to make a decent blend.

Serve it or store it in the freezer for 1-2 months. (For storing baby food, see page 63.)

TIP

If you don't have a blender, steam the peaches and mash them with the back of a fork.

Peach Blackberry Chia Pudding

 TIME: 10 MINS

This purée is full of vitamins, fiber, omega-3 fatty acids, protein, and several essential minerals and has a yummy taste your little one won't be able to resist.

MATERIAL

- 2 ripe peaches, skinned and stoned
- Handful of blackberries
- 1½ tbsp chia seeds, soaked
- 2 pitted dates
- ¼ tsp ground cinnamon
- Dash of coconut milk

CONSTRUCTION

Place the peaches, blackberries, dates, and ground cinnamon in a blender or food processor.

Purée until smooth, mix in the chia seeds, and add coconut milk if required.

Spinach Sweet Potato Blend  TIME: 15 MINS

MATERIAL

- A handful of spinach leaves
- ½ sweet potato, peeled and cubed

CONSTRUCTION

Bring a little water to the boil in a saucepan, add spinach leaves in a steamer basket, and cover with the lid for 5 minutes until tender.

Either steam the sweet potato similarly or put it in a saucepan with a little water and cook until tender.

Transfer the spinach leaves and sweet potato to a blender and blend until smooth.

Chickpeas and Carrot Blend  TIME: 20 MINS

Carrot is a great source of vitamin A, and adding chickpeas to it makes it more nutritious. This recipe is loaded with carbs, fiber, protein, and vitamins.

MATERIAL

- 1 cup canned/boiled chickpeas
- 1 large carrot, scrubbed and chopped
- 1 small onion, peeled and finely chopped
- 1 garlic clove, crushed
- Pinch of turmeric
- Pinch of ground cumin
- Pinch of ground cinnamon
- 1 to 2 tbsp olive oil

CONSTRUCTION

Heat olive oil in a saucepan over medium heat, add onion, and sauté until translucent. Add garlic, turmeric, cumin, cinnamon, carrot, and chickpeas, and fry for 30 seconds.

Now put ½ cup of water to cover the base of the saucepan and cover with a lid. Let it simmer for 10 to 15 minutes on low heat until carrots are tender.

Transfer to a food processor or blender and purée. Add cooking water for a thinner consistency. Serve or store in the freezer for up to 2 months.

Apple Oats Purée

 **TIME: 15 MINS**

Oats are a great source of carbs. Being a perfect blend of carbs, fiber, and vitamin C makes it a healthy meal for your little one.

MATERIAL

- ½ apple, peeled and cubed
- 6 tbsp rolled oats/quick oats
- 250 ml water

CONSTRUCTION

Put all the ingredients in a saucepan and let them simmer on medium heat.

With the help of a blender, purée the cooked mixture until smooth.

Add breast milk/formula or water for the desired consistency.

(Double the ingredients to make a large batch for freezing.) For freezing and storing the purée, see page 63.

Fruit Chia Pudding

 TIME: 10 MINS

This works with almost every sweet fruit. Look in your fridge for any ripe fruit and make a yummy pudding within minutes.

MATERIAL

- Raspberries (or any other ripe fruit)
- 60 ml coconut milk/cow's milk
- 1 to 2 tbsp chia seeds

CONSTRUCTION

Put the raspberries and milk in a blender. Purée until smooth.

Mix in the chia seeds and place the mixture in a refrigerator for a few hours.

Puddings can be kept for up to 42 hours in a refrigerator.

Potato Carrot Rice Purée

 TIME: 15 MINS

Make boring rice cereal into a healthy, tasty treat, great for your growing baby. Nutrients include fiber, vitamin K1, potassium, antioxidants, vitamin C, and complex carbohydrates.

MATERIAL

- ½ potato, peeled and cubed
- ½ carrot, peeled and cubed
- ½ cup rice
- 300ml water

CONSTRUCTION

Mix all the Material in a saucepan and bring to a simmer on medium heat.

When the potato and carrot are tender, blend the cooked mixture as much as required.

Water or milk can be added for the desired consistency.

Serve or store for later.

Zucchini and Pea Porridge

 TIME: 20 MINS

This porridge is packed with vitamin c, vitamin B-6, magnesium, fiber, potassium, and a hint of carbs.

MATERIAL

- 3 zucchini cut into chunks
- 1 cup of shelled peas (fresh or frozen)
- 1 cup rolled oats
- 1 ripe banana

CONSTRUCTION

Steam zucchini chunks and peas. Reserve the water. Put oats in a medium-sized saucepan and add 1 to 2 cups of water.

Cook for 8 to 12 minutes until the water has been absorbed and the oats are soft. Transfer all the Material to a blender and blend until smooth. Add reserved water if required for a runny consistency.

Breakfast

SERVING: 9 BARS

French Toast Bars

 **TIME: 15 MINS**

A quick breakfast recipe to put together for your tots and perfect food to start your baby-led-weaning journey since the eggy bread is super soft but firm enough to hold in their tiny hands.

MATERIAL

- 1 ripe mashed banana
- 2-3 white bread slices
- 60ml milk
- 1 large egg
- Knob of unsalted butter/1 tbsp olive oil
- ¼ tsp ground cinnamon (optional)
- 1tsp vanilla essence
- 1 tsp maple syrup (or honey, suitable for a 1-year-old)

CONSTRUCTION

Beat an egg in a shallow bowl, then add a dash of milk, maple syrup, puréed banana, cinnamon, and vanilla essence.

Grease a non-stick frying pan over medium heat.

Dip a slice of bread in the egg mixture and coat well on both sides. Place the eggy bread in the frying pan. Fry on both sides until brown.

Transfer to a cutting board and cut each slice into 3 bars. Serve with fruit. Delicious!

TO STORE

You can store leftovers in the refrigerator for 1 day in an airtight container or wrap them in foil to butter paper to prevent drying out.

SERVING: 1 ADULT, 1 KID

Spinach Omelet Swirls

 **TIME: 10 MINS**

This healthy and protein-loaded breakfast is perfect for your growing baby. It makes more fun for babies by making swirls out of dull omelets.

MATERIAL

- 3 eggs
- Handful of spinach leaves, washed and finely chopped
- 2½ tbsp grated cheddar cheese
- Pinch of white/black pepper to taste
- 2 tbsp olive oil/cooking oil or a knob of butter (unsalted)

CONSTRUCTION

Beat the eggs, add spinach leaves, cheddar cheese, and a pinch of pepper, and whisk.

Melt a knob of unsalted butter in a small, nonstick frying pan on medium heat.

Pour the mixture into the frying pan and fry until well-cooked on both sides.

Remove from pan and transfer to a cutting board. Cut into long strips and roll up, securing with a toothpick or skewer for a more finished look.

SERVING: 1 KID

Scrambled Egg

 **TIME: 10 MINS**

MATERIAL

- 1 egg
- 1 tbsp coriander leaves/parsley leaves, finely chopped
- Pinch of black pepper
- 2 tbsp grated cheddar cheese
- 2 tbsp chopped onion (optional)
- Knob of butter/2 tsp cooking oil

CONSTRUCTION

Melt the butter in a small frying pan on medium heat. Sauté the chopped onion until translucent.

Crack the egg onto the onions and toss. Add cheddar cheese and ½ tbsp finely chopped coriander leaves/parsley leaves and cook well.

Remove from pan when cooked and sprinkle with black pepper and the remaining chopped coriander/parsley leaves. Serve with toasted bread.

SERVING: 2 KIDS

Cooked Oats

 **TIME: 15 MINS**

A quick and healthy recipe for your little one to start the day.

MATERIAL

- 1 cup rolled oats
- Half a mango cut into chunks (any ripe fruit can be used)
- 2 to 3 tsp desiccated coconut
- Milk as much as desired
- Maple syrup to drizzle
- Fruit to garnish

CONSTRUCTION

Place rolled oats in a saucepan and add 1 cup of water. Cook on medium heat and let it simmer. Add mango chunks and desiccated coconut.

Cover with a lid for 5 minutes. Remove the pan when there is no water left.

Serve with fruit and maple syrup. Add milk for your desired consistency.

SERVING: 6 PANCAKES

Vegan Banana Oats Pancakes

 TIME: 15 MINS

This is a perfect recipe if your child is allergic to egg, wheat, or milk. It doesn't compromise on nutrients.

MATERIAL

- 1 large, ripe banana
- 1½ cups gluten-free rolled oats, finely ground and sieved
- 1 cup dairy-free milk (almond, coconut, etc.)
- 1 tsp vanilla extract
- ½ tsp baking powder
- Pinch of salt
- Maple syrup (or honey if child is 1 year old)
- 1 tsp ground flax seeds (optional)

CONSTRUCTION

Put oat flour in a medium bowl and add baking soda, a pinch of salt, and ground flax. Mix well and set aside.

Blend banana, milk, and vanilla extract together and pour into dry oat mixture. Fold until combined and smooth.

Grease a nonstick pan and heat it over medium heat.

Pour some batter into a nonstick pan. Make it round with the back of a spoon. When bubbles forms on the surface, flip it over. Remove from the pan when brown.

Serve with fruit, maple syrup, or honey.

TO STORE

Keep in an airtight container in the fridge and enjoy for up to 3 days.

Microwave or lightly fry again to make them fresh and warm.

> **TIP**
>
> For a perfectly round pancake:
>
> Use the biggest measuring spoon for ladling out the batter.

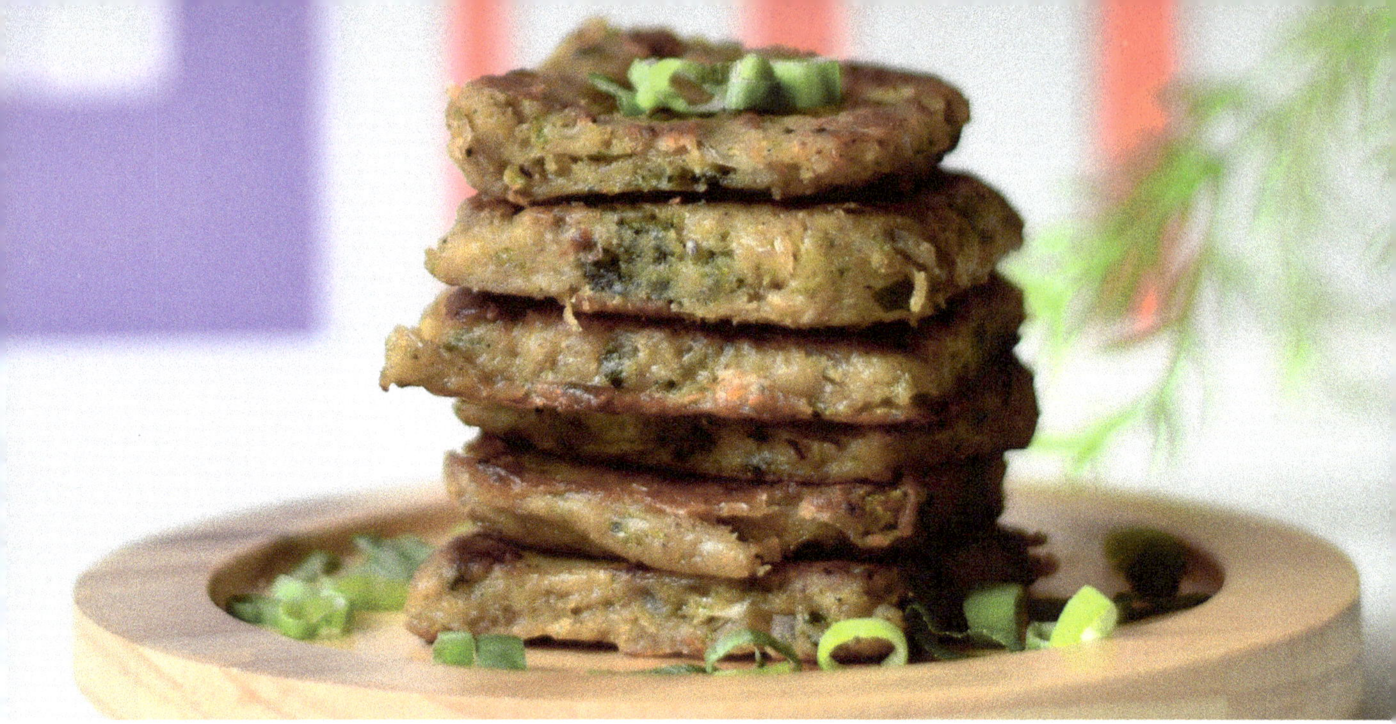

SERVING: 6 SQUARES

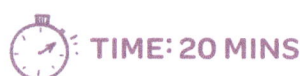

Vegan Zucchini Squares

TIME: 20 MINS

Serve these crispy squares as a healthy appetizer, freeze the leftovers, and serve for up to 2 months.

MATERIAL

- 1 large zucchini, shredded
- ½ cup broccoli florets (optional)
- 1 medium onion, finely chopped
- ½ tsp crushed garlic
- 2 tbsp parsley leaves
- ½ cup whole wheat flour
- ¼ cup chickpea flour
- ¼ tsp black pepper
- Pinch of salt
- ½ tsp baking powder
- Knob of butter/vegetable oil

CONSTRUCTION

Toss crushed garlic, onion, zucchini, and broccoli in hot oil or butter for a few minutes until half cooked.

Add these to the remaining ingredients in a large bowl and mix well.

The batter might be too thick or too thin depending on the water content of the zucchini. Add water if it is too stiff or add wheat flour if too runny.

Knead the batter and form into squares or circles. Place in the fridge for 1 hour before cooking. Shallow fry on medium heat until brown.

ANOTHER WAY

Grease a 6-inch baking tray and line it with butter paper. Pour the batter into the tray and bake for 15 minutes.

Transfer to a cutting board, cut into equal squares, and shallow fry on medium heat or air fry for crispy squares. Enjoy!

SERVING: 9 BARS

Spinach Eggy Bars

 **TIME: 15 MINS**

An easy-peasy recipe to make healthy finger food loaded with nutrients. Store in the fridge and let your baby enjoy for up to 2 days.

MATERIAL

- 3 slices of bread (with or without crust)
- Bunch of frozen or fresh baby spinach
- 2 tbsp grated cheddar cheese
- 1 large egg
- Pinch of white pepper
- Knob of butter or oil for greasing pan

CONSTRUCTION

Blend all the ingredients except bread slices in a blender until smooth.

Dip each slice of bread in the eggy mixture and coat both sides well.

Grease a frying pan and fry the coated bread over medium heat for a few minutes until golden brown. Transfer to a cutting board and cut each slice into 3 bars. Serve.

> **TIP**
> You can use other vegetables such as broccoli, carrot, or zucchini.

7 months to 9 months

Schematic Weekly Planner

week 1

	DAY 1	DAY 2	DAY 3	DAY 4	DAY 5	DAY 6	DAY 7
EARLY MORNING	Breast/ formula milk	Breast/ formula milk	Breast/ formula milk	Breast/ formula milk	Breast/ formula milk	Breast/ formula milk	Breast/ formula milk
BREAKFAST	Spinach eggy fingers	Scrambled egg	Oats pancakes	Vegan zucchini fritters	French toast fingers	Cooked oats	Spinach omelet coils
LUNCH	Breast/ formula milk	Breast/ formula milk	Breast/ formula milk	Breast/ formula milk	Breast/ formula milk	Breast/ formula milk	Breast/ formula milk
SNACKS	Broccoli potato blend	Pea and sweet potato	Apple peach apricot	Potato carrot rice	Chickpea and carrot	Fruit chia pudding	Rice cereal
DINNER	Breast/ formula milk	Breast/ formula milk	Breast/ formula milk	Breast/ formula milk	Breast/ formula milk	Breast/ formula milk	Breast/ formula milk

week 2

	DAY 1	DAY 2	DAY 3	DAY 4	DAY 5	DAY 6	DAY 7
EARLY MORNING	Breast/ formula milk	Breast/ formula milk	Breast/ formula milk	Breast/ formula milk	Breast/ formula milk	Breast/ formula milk	Breast/ formula milk
BREAKFAST	French toast fingers	Cooked oats	Vegan zucchini fritters	Scrambled egg	Rice cereal	Spinach eggy fingers	Oats pancakes
LUNCH	Breast/ formula milk	Breast/ formula milk	Breast/ formula milk	Breast/ formula milk	Breast/ formula milk	Breast/ formula milk	Breast/ formula milk
SNACKS	Spinach sweet potato blend	Broccoli small florets	Suji cereal	Banana fingers	Peach chia pudding	Apple fingers	Dragon and peach
DINNER	Breast/ formula milk	Breast/ formula milk	Breast/ formula milk	Breast/ formula milk	Breast/ formula milk	Breast/ formula milk	Breast/ formula milk

*Maintain the usual milk intake during the night.

LEVEL 3 – From 9 months to 12 months and beyond

Finger food to table food

Time has flown, and it's already three months since you started weaning your little one. Your baby can have three meals a day and he can eat nearly everything now, yet most babies' appetites wane and their weight gain slows down as they start to teethe. Nonetheless, in this phase, babies are more enthusiastic about taking charge of their food. They like to feed themselves rather than letting someone feed them. They're more likely to reject puréed foods but are willing to gobble finger foods. Aim at having most of your meals together as a family and serve food in a highchair. Your baby may be interested in observing you all eating and enjoy his meal, too.

Structure

This is a transition phase in which your baby's food is changing from finger food to table food. Be cautious in your use of salt and sugar. Your baby needs very little salt, less than 1g per day. And limit sugary treats to avoid tooth decay and overstimulation.

Breakfast

SERVING: 2 PYRAMIDS

Mango Toast Pyramid

 TIME: 15 MINS

Make your tot a little surprise breakfast. I bet he will be keen to see what's beneath the pyramid.

MATERIAL

- 3 slices of bread (with or without crusts)
- 1 ripe mango, peeled and mashed
- 60ml milk
- 1 large egg
- Pinch of saffron powder
- Knob of unsalted butter/ 1 tbsp olive oil
- 2 to 3 tsp desiccated coconut
- 1tsp maple syrup (or honey if 1 year old)

CONSTRUCTION

Beat an egg in a shallow bowl, add all the other ingredients and give it a good mix. Grease a frying pan over medium heat.

Dip each slice of bread in egg mixture and coat well on both sides. Place the eggy bread in the frying pan. Fry on both sides until cooked and remove. Cut the bread slices in half diagonally.

Take three of the cut slices and stack them to form a pyramid. (Use half a toothpick to join corners if stabilization is required.)

Hide slices of fruit or veggies underneath the pyramid.

FINGER FOOD

Cut the slice of bread into fingers lengthwise and serve with fruits. Delicious!

SERVING: 3 DOUBLE DECKS

Double-decker Jammie Dodger French Toast

 **TIME: 20 MINS**

This can be served as a special treat to your kids at the breakfast table. Yummylicious!

MATERIAL

- 6 slices of bread
- ½ cup milk
- 2 eggs
- 1½ tsp vanilla essence
- 1tsp maple syrup
- 3 tbsp sugar-free raspberry jam (or any fruit jam) (or honey if it's for a one-year-old)
- Knob of unsalted butter/2 tbsp cooking oil

CONSTRUCTION

In a medium-sized bowl, crack an egg and add a dash of milk, vanilla essence, and maple syrup. Wisk together until well combined.

Grease a large frying pan over medium heat.

Dip each slice of bread in the egg mixture, coating both sides well, and place in the frying pan. Fry on both sides until brown and remove from pan.

Spread the raspberry jam on 3 slices. Using a cookie cutter, cut out the middle of the other 3 slices.

Sandwich together, garnish with your favorite berries and serve. Yum!

SERVING: 3 PUFFS

Boiled Egg Puff Pastry Pockets

 **TIME: 25 MINS**

A delightful breakfast treat. Great to pack into a lunch box for daycare, nursery, or school.

MATERIAL

- 3 squares ready-to-use puff pastry, 4"x4"
- 1 boiled egg
- 1 beaten egg for egg wash
- Pinch of black pepper
- Pinch of oregano (optional)
- 2 tbsp grated cheddar cheese (optional)

CONSTRUCTION

Preheat the oven to 220 degrees, line a baking tray, and set it aside.

Place store-bought puff pastry squares on a floured surface so they don't stick.

Cut the boiled egg into three slices and place one on the middle of each piece of puff pastry. Now fold and overlap the two opposite corners over the boiled egg. As shown in the illustrations, fold the bottom corner over the other two flaps. Wash with beaten egg and pop into the middle section of the oven.

Bake for 15 minutes until puffed and shiny golden brown. Serve hot or pack in the lunchbox for on the go.

SERVING: 1 ADULT, 1 KID

Pink Pancake Pile

 **TIME: 20 MINS**

A pop of natural strawberry color and a slightly different flavor from plain pancakes change the mood of your little one.

MATERIAL

- 8 tbsp all-purpose flour
- ½ tsp baking powder
- 1 tbsp granulated sugar
- Pinch of salt
- 1 cup milk
- 1 egg
- 1 tsp strawberry-flavored syrup
- ¼ tsp natural red food dye (optional)
- Knob of unsalted butter/2 tbsp cooking oil
- Fruit for serving
- Maple syrup (or honey if one year old) for serving

CONSTRUCTION

In a large bowl, mix all the dry ingredients.

In another bowl, whisk together the milk, egg, strawberry syrup, and red food coloring. Pour this mixture into the dry ingredients and mix well.

Heat a nonstick pan over medium heat and grease it.

Pour some batter into the nonstick pan. When bubbles start to show, flip the pancake. Remove from the pan when cooked.

Serve with fruit, maple syrup, or honey.

TIP

For perfectly round pancakes: Use the biggest measuring scoop for ladling out the batter.

For natural food colorants, see page 28.

Textured Omelet

SERVING: 2 KIDS

 TIME: 15 MINS

MATERIAL

- 2 eggs
- Knob of unsalted butter/2 tbsp cooking oil
- Pinch white pepper or black pepper
- 1 tbsp capsicum, chopped
- 1 tbsp onion, chopped
- 1 tbsp tomato, chopped
- 1 tbsp freshly chopped coriander leaves
- 2 tbsp grated cheddar cheese
- 1 tbsp cream cheese
- 1 tbsp chopped chicken sausages (use occasionally if your kid is 12 to 24 months old)

CONSTRUCTION

Beat 2 eggs in a medium-sized bowl and add all the other ingredients.

Grease a frying pan on medium heat and pour in the eggy mixture. Cover and cook over low heat for 5 minutes. Remove when cooked.

Garnish with some freshly chopped coriander leaves, and serve!

SERVING: 1 ADULT, 1 KID

Frittata

 TIME: 25 MINS

Another scrumptious recipe for the breakfast table, including healthy veggies.

MATERIAL

- 3 large eggs
- Handful of baby spinach, chopped
- Bunch of fresh coriander leaves, chopped
- 1tsp spring onions or onions, finely chopped
- Bunch of broccoli florets, chopped
- ½ tomato, chopped
- 1tbsp mushrooms, diced
- 1 tbsp capsicum, chopped
- 2 tbsp of dairy cream
- 2 tbsp mozzarella cheese, grated
- 2 tbsp cheddar cheese, grated
- 1 clove garlic, minced
- ½ tsp black pepper
- Knob of unsalted butter/3 tbsp cooking oil

(You can skip any of the above veggies not available in your fridge.)

CONSTRUCTION

Beat eggs with dairy cream and black pepper until well mixed and set aside.

Pre-cook all the above vegetables by sauteing and steaming in a medium-size nonstick pan over low-medium heat. (You can also use a stainless steel pan.)

Pour the egg mixture over the veggies and fold, add grated cheese, and cover with a lid for 2-5 minutes, allowing the cheese to melt and the egg to be well done.

TO BAKE

Pour the egg mixture over cooked veggies and fold, sprinkle cheese on top and bake in preheated oven for 10-15 minutes.

Frittata enriched with lots of nutrients is ready to serve!

SERVING: 1 ADULT, 2 KIDS

Overnight Oats

 **TIME: 10 MINS**

Prepare this before you go to sleep or a few hours before and have a wholesome breakfast for you and your baby the next day. I call it a lazy breakfast!

MATERIAL

- 2 cups rolled oats or quick oats (ground if desired)
- 1 cup milk
- 5 to 6 strawberries or any berries
- 1 tbsp whole chia seeds/1½ tbsp ground chia seeds
- 1 sliced banana (for topping)
- A handful of chopped blueberries
- 2 tbsp desiccated coconut
- Chopped dried fruit
- Maple syrup (or honey suitable for a 1-year-old)

CONSTRUCTION

Blend strawberries (or any available fruit) and milk. Add rolled oats and chia seeds and mix well.

Keep in refrigerator overnight.

Garnish with your favorite fruit or sliced banana and chopped blueberries.

SERVING: 6 WAFFLE SQUARES

Belgian Chocolate Chip Waffle Squares

 **TIME: 25 MINS**

A waffle feast on the weekend for the whole family to enjoy! Double or triple the recipe for storing and freezing. (Serve only occasionally.)

MATERIAL

- 1½ cups all-purpose flour
- 1 cup white sugar
- 100g unsalted butter
- ½ tsp baking powder
- 200ml milk
- ¼ tsp salt
- 1½ tbsp Belgian chocolate chips
- ½ tsp vanilla-flavored sugar or 1tsp vanilla extract
- 2 eggs, separated
- Whipped cream or vanilla ice cream (for topping)
- Strawberry chunks (for topping)

CONSTRUCTION

Beat egg whites until foamy and set aside.

Beat egg yolks together, gradually add all the other ingredients, and fold in the foamy egg whites at the end.

Grease and preheat the waffle tray before pouring on the batter.

Let each waffle cook for 3 to 4 minutes until golden brown.

Serve with vanilla ice cream and sprinkled with chocolate chips. Yummylicious!

SERVING: 5 WAFFLE SQUARES

Lemon Vanilla Waffle Squares

 **TIME: 25 MINS**

MATERIAL

- 2 cups all-purpose flour
- 4 tbsp white sugar
- 2 tsp baking soda
- 2 eggs, separated
- 2 tsp lemon zest or 1 tsp lemon syrup
- 1 tsp vanilla extract
- ¼ tsp salt
- 2 cups milk
- 6 tbsp melted butter (unsalted)
- Fruit for serving
- Maple syrup (or honey suitable for 1-year-old)

CONSTRUCTION

Beat egg whites until foamy and set aside. Whisk all dry ingredients (flour, sugar, baking soda, salt) in another bowl and set aside.

In a separate bowl, whisk egg yolks, lemon zest, vanilla extract, and milk, transfer this to the flour mixture, and mix well.

Add melted butter and fold in foamy egg whites until well combined. Pour the batter onto a greased, pre-heated waffle tray and cook according to the manufacturer's instructions until golden brown. Serve hot!

SERVING: 4-5 WAFFLES

Chaffle Squares

 **TIME: 25 MINS**

Who knew you could make mouthwatering cheese waffles with a simple waffle maker? They are a perfect savory loaded with cheese – we call them chaffles!

MATERIAL

- 100g unsalted butter, melted
- 2 eggs
- 1 cup milk
- 1½ cups all-purpose flour
- 1 cup grated cheddar or mozzarella cheese; add more if required
- 1 tsp baking powder

CONSTRUCTION

Mix flour and baking powder in a bowl and set aside.

In another bowl, whisk egg, add milk, gradually add the dry mixture, and combine until no lumps are left.

Add melted butter and mix well.

Pour the batter into the greased and pre-heated waffle maker and let it cook for 5-8 minutes until golden brown and crunchy. Serve hot.

SERVING: 1 SANDWICH

Cheese Egg Toast

 **TIME: 15 MINS**

Looking for easy yet flavorsome toast? This recipe is for you and your little one.

MATERIAL

- 2 slices of bread (whole grain or white)
- 1 egg
- 2 tbsp shredded cheddar or mozzarella cheese
- Black pepper to taste
- Pinch of oregano

CONSTRUCTION

Preheat the oven to 180 degrees.

In a bowl, whisk egg, cheese, black pepper, and oregano. Spread on each slice of the bread and sandwich. You can also spread the mixture on the outer surfaces if you like.

Bake for 10 to 12 minutes until cooked. Cut into strips before serving. Enjoy!

TIP

You can also toast each slice of bread separately without sandwiching.

If don't want to bake in the oven, place the toast in a pan, cover with the lid, and cook on low heat until golden brown. Serve hot.

SERVING: 1 ADULT, 1 KID

Crepes

 **TIME: 25 MINS**

I never knew they were so delicious until I tried them. These crepes are the tastiest treat for your baby and toddler to enjoy on the weekend.

MATERIAL

- 8 tbsp all-purpose flour
- 1 tbsp granulated sugar
- Pinch of salt
- 1½ cups milk
- 1 egg
- Knob of unsalted butter for cooking
- Fruit for serving
- Maple syrup or honey for serving
- Cooking oil for greasing

CONSTRUCTION

In a large bowl, mix all dry ingredients (all-purpose flour, sugar, and salt).

In another bowl, whisk the milk and egg, pour into the dry ingredients, and fold in well. Keep the batter at room temperature for 10 to 15 minutes until slightly bubbly on top.

Pre-heat a nonstick pan over medium heat and grease it.

Pour a little batter into the pan. Flip when bubbles form. Remove from the pan when golden brown.

Serve with fruit, maple syrup, or honey.

> **TIP**
> Use a scoop for pouring and spreading the batter evenly in the pan.

SERVING: 4 VEG MUFFINS

Egg Muffins

 **TIME: 25 MINS**

A super-duper hit recipe to try, loaded with veggies. Freezer friendly and lets your tots enjoy them for up to 2 months.

MATERIAL

- 2 large eggs
- A handful of baby spinach, finely chopped
- 2 tbsp tomato, chopped
- 2 tbsp capsicum, chopped
- 2 tbsp onion, chopped
- 3 tbsp grated cheddar cheese(optional)
- 1 tbsp coriander leaves, finely chopped
- Pinch of salt and black pepper
- Melted butter to grease

CONSTRUCTION

Preheat oven to 180 degrees. In a large bowl, whisk all the ingredients together.

Grease a muffin tray or use butter paper liners if you prefer.

Pour out the mixture and place the tray in the oven for 10 to 15 minutes until well done. (You can sprinkle some extra grated cheddar cheese on top of the mixture.)

Wait for a few minutes before taking the muffins out of the tray.

Double or triple the recipe for a large batch.

SERVING: 3 BREAD PIZZAS

Bread Pizza

 **TIME: 25 MINS**

Who said we can't have pizza in the morning? Here's trouble-free yet appetizing pizza on your breakfast table for your toddler.

MATERIAL

- 3 slices of bread
- 5 tbsp grated cheddar or mozzarella cheese
- 4 tbsp capsicum, chopped
- 5 tbsp tomato, chopped
- 8 sliced and pitted black olives
- 3 tbsp chopped onion
- Pinch of paprika and oregano

CONSTRUCTION

Brush a nonstick pan lightly with a few drops of oil. Lightly toast the bread slices on both sides and remove them from the pan before the bread begins to harden.

Spread the bread with pizza sauce, ketchup, or any sauce you prefer. Layer with onion, capsicum, tomato, and olives. Sprinkle with grated mozzarella or cheddar cheese, as much you desire.

Sprinkle with herbs or paprika if you like and transfer the slices to the pan. Cover the pan and let the cheddar cheese melt on low heat. (Make sure you don't burn the bottom of the bread.) Serve when the cheese has melted.

TO BAKE

Pop in preheated oven for 10 minutes at 180 degrees.

> **TIP**
> You can also add grilled or fried chicken pieces to the veggies.

SERVING: 1 KID

Egg Mince

 **TIME: 15 MINS**

An Asian recipe adding flavor to your simple scrambled egg.

MATERIAL

- 1 egg
- 2 medium tomatoes, chopped
- A handful of coriander leaves
- ½ tsp coriander powder
- ¼ tsp black pepper
- Pinch of salt
- Knob of butter/2 tbsp cooking oil

CONSTRUCTION

In a medium-sized pan, melt the butter on medium heat, add the tomato, salt, pepper, and coriander powder and mix well.

Cover with the lid on low heat until the tomato is tender. Mash the tomatoes into a paste and stir until the oil separates. Break the egg into the pan, add coriander leaves, and mix well.

Fry until the egg is well done. Serve with paratha!

SERVING: 10 MINI DONUTS

Pancake Mini Donuts

 **TIME: 20 MINS**

A delightful morning treat for your little one, switching from dull pancakes to exciting donuts.

MATERIAL

- 8 tbsp all-purpose flour
- 2 tbsp granulated sugar
- ½ tsp baking powder
- ¼ tsp baking soda
- Pinch of salt
- ½ cup milk
- 1 egg
- 1 tsp vanilla extract
- Nonstick cooking spray
- Fruit and sprinkles for topping
- Melted chocolate for topping

CONSTRUCTION

Preheat the oven to 180 degrees.

In a large bowl, mix all dry Material (flour, sugar, baking soda, baking powder, and salt).

In another bowl, beat an egg together with the milk and vanilla extract. Pour the mixture into the dry ingredients and fold in until well mixed.

Spray a donut pan lightly with nonstick spray (or brush it with melted butter or cooking oil).

Pour the batter into the donut cavities. Wipe off the middle of the donut cavities as the batter will drip across as you pour. (You can use a piping bag to avoid getting it everywhere.)

Bake for 10-15 minutes until the batter is cooked. Wait for 10 minutes before removing.

Serve with your favorite topping!!

> **TIP**
>
> Insert a toothpick into the donut to check whether it is fully cooked. If the toothpick comes out dry, it means they are ready.
>
> You can add unsweetened cocoa powder for a chocolate flavor.

SERVING: 1 ADULT, 1 KID

Egg Roll

 TIME: 25 MINS

Yummy and tasty rolls loaded with healthy veggies, giving a unique taste and texture.

MATERIAL

- 3 eggs
- 1 tbsp carrot, finely chopped
- 1 tbsp onion, finely chopped
- 1 tbsp spring onion, chopped
- 1 tbsp milk
- Pinch of salt
- Pinch of black pepper

CONSTRUCTION

Crack eggs into a bowl, add milk and salt, and whisk until well combined.

Add chopped carrot, onion, spring onion, and black pepper and mix well.

Grease a pan with cooking oil. Pour in half the egg mixture and cook on low heat until almost cooked.

Roll the omelet halfway up to the middle of the pan, grease the pan if needed, pour 1/4 of the egg mixture into the space and cook.

Roll up the omelet halfway again, and move the egg roll to the center of the pan.

Pour the remaining egg mixture into the space in the pan and cook.

Roll when cooked. Gently transfer to a cutting board and cut into bite-size pieces.

> **TIP**
> Use a silicone spatula that will help to roll the egg without breaking it!

SERVING: 2 KIDS

Brown Rice Cereal

 **TIME: 20 MINS**

A satisfying and filling cereal to start the day.

MATERIAL

- ¼ cup ground brown rice
- 2 cups water
- Applesauce/mango/sweet potato
- Milk for serving

CONSTRUCTION

Bring the water to a boil in a saucepan.

Add ground brown rice and stir until desired consistency.

Serve with any favorite add-ons. Add milk if needed.

SERVING: 2 KIDS

Egg Paratha Roll

 **TIME: 15 MINS**

A roasted flatbread layered with soft egg, making it a healthy and yummy breakfast for your little one to delight in!

MATERIAL

- 1 paratha (frozen or ready to use)
- 1 large egg
- 1 tbsp grated cheddar cheese
- Pinch of pepper
- 1½ tbsp mayonnaise
- 1 large lettuce leaf, finely chopped
- 1tbsp ketchup (optional)

CONSTRUCTION

Beat an egg, then add cheddar cheese and a pinch of pepper. Fry in pan, cook on both sides, and transfer to a plate.

Heat the paratha, spread with mayonnaise, sprinkle with chopped lettuce, top with the cooked egg, drizzle with ketchup, and roll up the paratha.

Cut the slices of paratha about 1-inch thick, secure with a toothpick (optional), and enjoy!

SERVING: 10 BARS

Cereal Energy Bars

 TIME: 25 MINS

A great option for picky eaters and a perfect breakfast on the run!

MATERIAL

- ½ cup almond butter or peanut butter
- ½ cup puffed rice (brown or white)
- ½ cup maple syrup (or honey if for one-year-old)
- 1 cup old-fashioned rolled oats, toasted
- ½ cup crushed or grated almonds
- ½ cup puffed quinoa or millet (optional)
- ¼ cup roughly chopped dried blueberries
- ¼ cup roughly chopped dried cranberries
- ¼ cup roughly chopped dried apricot
- Pinch of salt

CONSTRUCTION

Heat the almond butter in a saucepan, add maple syrup, and stir until combined.

In another bowl, mix all the dry ingredients, pour in the almond butter, and mix well.

Grease a 6-inch square tray and pour in the cereal mixture. Press it down lightly with wet hands and level it.

Cool for an hour in a refrigerator. Transfer the chilled mixture to a cutting board and cut it into bars.

TO STORE

Keep in an airtight container and enjoy for up to 5 days.

Main course

SERVING: 12 SPHERES

Chicken Spheres

 **TIME: 30 MINS**

Croquettes are a versatile dish you can fill with anything your heart desires – minced meat, veggies, or cheese. A delicious recipe for kids to enjoy!

MATERIAL

- 1 chicken thigh, boiled and shredded
- ½ medium onion, chopped
- 3 potatoes, peeled, steamed/boiled
- ½ cup crispy breadcrumbs
- 1 garlic clove, crushed
- 1 egg
- ½ tsp ground cumin
- ½ tsp ground nutmeg
- Pinch of salt
- ½ tsp black pepper
- Oil for cooking

CONSTRUCTION

Heat 2 tablespoons of oil in a frying pan on medium heat. Sauté crushed garlic, add onion, and toss until translucent.

Add shredded chicken and spices and fry for 5 minutes. Remove the pan and set it aside.

Put the potato in a bowl and mash.

Add the cooked chicken and mix well. Add some breadcrumbs if sticky.

Apply a little cooking oil to your palms and shape the mixture into small balls.

Place the breadcrumbs on a shallow plate and whisk the egg into a small bowl.

Roll each ball in breadcrumbs, dip in egg, then coat again with breadcrumbs until completely covered.

Refrigerate for 1 to 2 hours to preserve their shape.

Deep fry over medium heat and serve with your favorite sauce.

SERVING: 2 ADULTS, 2 KIDS

Lentil Soup

 **TIME: 20 MINS**

If you're looking to lighten up your baby's meals or warm him up with a steaming bowl of soup, this healthy recipe is for you!

MATERIAL

- ½ cup red lentils
- ½ medium tomato, diced
- ½ medium carrot, peeled and diced
- ½ medium onion, chopped
- 1 tbsp olive oil
- 1 tsp garlic, minced
- ½ tsp ground cumin
- ¼ tsp black pepper
- ¼ tsp turmeric powder

CONSTRUCTION

Heat the olive oil in a pot over medium heat. Add onion and garlic and stir well. Add all the other ingredients.

Give it a good mix and add 3 cups of water. Cover with the lid for 30 minutes and let it simmer over low-medium heat.

Purée the cooked mixture in a food processor or blender. Transfer the purée back to the pot and cook for another 15 minutes over medium-high heat (uncovered). Add water if required.

Stir well and remove the pot when it reaches the desired consistency. Garnish with herbs such as parsley or coriander.

*Parents can add salt later if desired.

SERVING: 12 CUTLETS

Potato Cutlets

 **TIME: 20 MINS**

This is the crispy version of my ever-popular potato cutlets. We form mashed potato into balls or other shapes, coat them in breadcrumbs, and fry them until crispy and golden. These potato cutlets can be served for lunch or dinner or as a side dish.

MATERIAL

- 4 medium potatoes, peeled and boiled
- A handful of mint leaves, finely chopped
- A handful of coriander leaves, or parsley, finely chopped
- 1 tbsp chopped spring onion (optional)
- Pinch of salt
- ½ tsp coriander powder
- Pinch of red chili powder
- ½ tsp whole coriander seeds, crushed
- ½ tsp ground cumin
- 2 tbsp grated cheddar cheese (optional)
- 3 tbsp cooking oil

CONSTRUCTION

In a bowl, mash the potatoes with a masher. Add all the herbs and spices, mix well, and knead. Form any shape you wish.

Place the cutlets in a freezer for 10 to 15 minutes before frying to preserve their shape.

Heat the oil in a nonstick frying pan and shallow fry the cutlets until golden brown. Bon appétit!

SERVING: 8 SKEWERS

Chicken Skewers

 TIME: 35 MINS

Make sure that you put chicken skewers on your list of delicious things to grill right away for your baby. Their tastebuds are going to be missing out if you don't give these a try.

MATERIAL

- 1 chicken breast
- 1 tbsp ginger garlic paste
- Pinch of salt
- ½ tsp white pepper
- 1 tbsp soy sauce
- 1 tbsp vinegar
- 1 tbsp mustard powder
- 1 capsicum cut into even chunks
- 1 tomato, cut into even chunks
- 1 onion, cut into even chunks
- Cooking spray

CONSTRUCTION

Cut chicken breast into equally sized cubes. Transfer to a bowl. Add ginger-garlic paste, vinegar, soy sauce, salt, white pepper, and mustard powder. Mix well and marinate chicken for 15 minutes. Thread the chicken pieces and vegetables onto skewers.

Heat a grill pan over medium heat, grease with cooking spray, and place the skewers in the pan. Let them cook on low heat. Turn after 5-10 minutes and brush with oil if required.

Remove when the chicken is tender. Serve hot!

SERVING: 9 FRITTERS

Zucchini Fritters

 **TIME: 25 MINS**

These fritters are unbelievably easy to make and the perfect way to sneak in some healthy zucchini.

MATERIAL

- 2 medium-sized zucchini, shredded
- 1 egg
- 6 tbsp oats flour
- 2 tbsp spring onion, chopped
- 2 tbsp grated cheddar cheese
- Pinch of salt
- ¼ tsp black pepper
- ½ tsp oregano
- ½ tsp coriander powder
- Olive oil for frying

CONSTRUCTION

Squeeze out all the excess liquid from the zucchini. (Place the grated zucchini on a clean cloth and squeeze out the water.)

In a bowl, mix all the ingredients well, then form into small, flat patties.

Shallow fry immediately in a frying pan over medium-high heat until golden brown. You can also bake them or air fry them in an air fryer.

SERVING: 2 ADULTS, 2 KIDS

Aloo Paratha Mini Sheets

 **TIME: 45 MINS**

The best part of making parathas is that you can serve them for breakfast, lunch, or even as a snack. Aloo parathas taste delicious.

MATERIAL

- 4 potatoes, peeled and boiled
- A handful of mint leaves, finely chopped
- A handful of coriander leaves, or parsley, finely chopped
- Salt to taste
- ½ tsp coriander powder
- ¼ tsp black pepper
- ½ tsp whole coriander seeds, crushed
- ½ tsp ground cumin
- 2 cups wholewheat flour
- 2 tbsp ghee or unsalted butter
- 3 tbsp cooking oil

CONSTRUCTION

Place flour, salt, ghee, and water in a bowl and knead into a dough. Cover and keep aside.

In another bowl, mash the potatoes with the help of a masher.

Add the herbs and spices. Mix well, knead, and set aside.

Take a small piece of dough, roll it into a ball, dust it with wholewheat flour, and with the help of a rolling pin, roll it into a round shape like roti/chapati.

Place the potato stuffing on half of the flat dough, then fold the other half over the stuffing. Press and seal the edges with your fingertips or the back of a fork. (Brushing a little water on the edges of the circle helps to seal them.)

Place the paratha on a hot skillet (Tawa) and flip when half-cooked. Brush with some cooking oil or ghee/butter and flip again and cook until it is nicely golden brown.

Bon appétit!

> **TIP**
> If the dough looks dry or feels hard, add a few tablespoons of water to portions and knead again. Sometimes the dough looks sticky, but as you continue to knead, the flour absorbs the water, and the stickiness goes away.

SERVING: 2 ADULTS, 1 KID

Chinese Fried Rice

 TIME: 25 MINS

This Chinese fried rice is a healthy toddler and baby meal. Filled with veggies, protein, and a ton of flavor, this easy lunch or dinner is great for the whole family. It's perfect for transitioning from baby-led weaning (finger foods) to table food.

MATERIAL

- ½ chicken breast, finely chopped
- 1 carrot, peeled and finely chopped
- 1 spring onion, chopped, with white bulb separated
- 1 medium capsicum, chopped
- ¼ cabbage, finely chopped (optional)
- 1 tbsp ginger garlic paste
- 1 tbsp garlic powder
- ½ tsp black pepper
- ½ tsp white pepper
- ½ tsp Chinese salt
- 2 tbsp vinegar
- ½ tsp chili sauce (optional)
- 2 tsp soy sauce
- 2 cups white rice
- 3 tbsp cooking oil

CONSTRUCTION

Marinating

Place chopped chicken in a bowl, add garlic powder, black pepper, white pepper, Chinese salt, vinegar, soy sauce, and salt, and mix well. Cover and marinate for 15 minutes.

Rice

Boil the rice, add salt to taste, drain the water when the rice is three-quarters cooked, and set aside.

Frying

Grease a large nonstick frying pan with cooking oil, add marinated chicken, and cook until tender. Remove it onto a plate and set aside.

Add chopped white bulb of spring onion to the pan and sauté for a few seconds.

Add carrots, capsicum, and cabbage and mix well.

Add ginger garlic paste, black and white pepper, Chinese salt, vinegar, and chili sauce, cover with the lid for 2 minutes, and fry.

Add boiled rice and chopped green spring onion and fry for a few seconds.

Add soy sauce, stir, and serve.

Easy-peasy Pasta

SERVING: 2 KIDS

 **TIME: 20 MINS**

This easy-peasy pasta is a nutritious and flavorful meal for babies and toddlers. It's great for baby-led weaning or the finger food stage, 7 months and up.

MATERIAL

- ½ cup pasta (whole-grain pasta can also be used)
- 1½ cups chicken broth
- ½ medium capsicum, finely chopped
- ½ carrot, shredded
- ½ cup frozen peas
- 2 tbsp grated cheddar cheese
- 1 tbsp butter
- 1 tbsp heavy cream
- Pinch of salt
- ¼ tsp black pepper

CONSTRUCTION

Place a medium-sized saucepan over medium heat and add broth, pasta, carrot, capsicum, peas, and salt. Let it simmer, stirring frequently, until al dente.

Add butter, cream, cheddar cheese, and pepper and mix well until combined. A creamy bowl of pasta is ready to serve!

SERVING: 2 KIDS

Broccoli Pasta

 **TIME: 20 MINS**

Who knew you could make something so tasty with broccoli, pasta, and not much else? Broccoli pasta is a little bit cheesy and a whole lot of yum for your little one.

MATERIAL

- ½ cup broccoli florets, chopped (frozen can be used)
- 2 tbsp asparagus, chopped (optional)
- ½ cup boiled and shredded chicken (optional)
- ½ cup short pasta, boiled
- 1 tsp ginger garlic paste
- 2 tbsp grated cheese (mozzarella or cheddar)
- 1 tbsp heavy cream
- Pinch of black pepper to taste

CONSTRUCTION

Sauté broccoli and asparagus, add ginger garlic paste, boiled chicken, and black pepper and toss for a few seconds.

Add pasta, cream, and cheese. Give it a good mix, and broccoli pasta is ready to serve!

SERVING: 1 ADULT, 2 KIDS

Potato Spinach Savory

 **TIME: 20 MINS**

Potato spinach is one of those simple, Asian, homely sorts of recipes that every household should keep in their repertoire.

MATERIAL

- 1 tbsp onion, chopped
- 1 tsp ginger garlic paste
- 1 medium potato, cut into even chunks
- 2 handfuls spinach leaves, washed and finely chopped
- Pinch of salt
- ½ tsp coriander powder
- Pinch of red chili powder
- Pinch of turmeric powder
- 3 tbsp cooking oil

CONSTRUCTION

Fry onion over medium heat until golden brown. Add ginger-garlic paste and stir. Add potato chunks and stir for 5 minutes then add spinach leaves and all the spices.

Give it a good mix and cover with the lid for 10-15 minutes over low heat until potato is tender. Remove the lid and stir again on medium heat for a few minutes more.

Potato spinach savory is ready to serve with roti or rice.

Cheese Spheres

SERVING: 10 SPHERES

 **TIME: 20 MINS**

Just like any rich appetizer, cheese spheres are flavorful, so a couple of bites will satisfy your baby.

MATERIAL

- 3 potatoes, peeled and boiled
- 3 tbsp breadcrumbs
- Pinch of salt
- ¼ tsp black pepper
- ½ tsp Italian herbs
- 1 tbsp coriander leaves, chopped
- 1 tsp garlic paste
- Bowl of corn starch for coating
- Cooking oil for frying
- For cheese stuffing
- 10 cheese cubes, ½ inch in size (cheddar or mozzarella)
- ¼ tsp black pepper
- ½ tsp Italian herbs
- ¼ allspice

CONSTRUCTION

Mash the potatoes until lump-free. Add breadcrumbs, black pepper, Italian herbs, chopped coriander, garlic paste, and a pinch of salt.

Mix well and knead into a big dough ball. The dough shouldn't be too sticky or too dry. Divide the dough into 9 or 10 equal spheres (balls) and set aside.

Toss together the cheddar cheese cubes, allspice, Italian herbs, and pepper.

Press each mashed potato sphere on your palm or butter paper and form it into a small round disc. Don't make it too thin.

Place the cheese cubes in the middle, cover the sides over, and form into a sphere again. Coat each ball with corn starch. (Mixture might tear, but that's okay; just roll it up into a ball again.)

Heat the oil in a deep pan, gently transfer the spheres into the oil, and deep fry over medium heat until golden brown.

> **TIP**
> After placing the spheres in the oil, don't move them for 30-60 seconds or they will break up.

SERVING: 2 KIDS

Mutton Brown

TIME: 40 MINS

Try my mom's popular dish. This mutton brown recipe requires only basic ingredients for a delicious and flavorsome meal for your toddler. This hearty dish is especially for babies who prefer a little spicy fare on their taste buds.

MATERIAL

- ½ kg boneless mutton chunks
- 1 tbsp yogurt
- ½ tsp garam masala
- 1 tbsp ginger garlic paste
- 1 tsp coriander seeds, ground
- 1 tsp cumin powder
- ½ green chili, chopped
- 1 tsp pomegranate seed powder (anaar dana)
- Pinch of salt
- 2 tbsp cooking oil

CONSTRUCTION

Seasoning

Mix cumin powder, ground pomegranate seeds, and ground coriander seeds in a small bowl and set aside.

Boil mutton chunks in a saucepan, add yogurt, salt, ginger garlic paste, and garam masala. Let it boil for 20 to 30 minutes until mutton is tender and the water has evaporated.

Heat cooking oil in a frying pan, add chili, and sauté until crispy. Transfer the boiled mutton to the frying pan and fry for few seconds on medium heat. Sprinkle 2 pinches of spice from the seasoning bowl and fry for 2 more minutes. Remove. Garnish with remaining seasoning and coriander leaves.

TO STORE

You can store boiled mutton in a freezer for 2 months.

SERVING: 1 ADULT, 2 KIDS

Chicken Gravy

 **TIME: 20 MINS**

Simple chicken gravy. Easy, quick, tasty chicken gravy with fewer spices that goes well with rice. This simple chicken gravy recipe is our family favorite, and it needs only simple ingredients that are sure to be in your pantry! This chicken gravy can be given to babies from 8 months after introducing chicken separately.

MATERIAL

- 1 medium chicken breast, cubed
- 1 capsicum, diced
- 2 tomatoes, sliced
- A handful of coriander leaves
- ½ tsp black pepper
- Pinch of salt
- ¼ tsp garam masala
- ½ tsp coriander powder
- 1 tbsp ginger garlic paste
- 3 – 4 tbsp cooking oil

CONSTRUCTION

Heat the oil in a saucepan over medium heat, add chicken, and stir for a few seconds. Add ginger-garlic paste and fry. Cover with the lid for 5 minutes over low heat.

Add salt, pepper, garam masala, and coriander powder and mix well.

When chicken water dries add tomatoes and capsicum and cover for 8-10 minutes. Add fresh coriander leaves and stir well until oil separates. Serve with white rice or fresh roti.

Falafel

SERVING: 12 BALLS

 **TIME: 20 MINS**

The best falafel sphere near you? It's right in your kitchen! This recipe is crispy on the outside, moist on the inside, garlicky, with lots of warm spices like cumin and coriander, and has the perfect texture.

MATERIAL

- 2 cups dry chickpeas (don't use canned)
- 1 medium onion, chopped
- ½ tsp ground cumin
- 1 tsp ground coriander
- Small bunch of parsley
- ¼ tsp black pepper
- 1½ garlic cloves, crushed

CONSTRUCTION

Soak dry chickpeas in a big bowl with lots of water for 8 hours. Don't cover them.

Drain all the water and transfer the chickpeas to a food processor or blender. Add onion, garlic, cumin, coriander, parsley, and black pepper and blend until well combined. (Add a splash of water if needed.)

Refrigerate for one hour. Press a small portion on your wet or oily palm and shape it. Coat in flour before deep frying. Falafel must float when dropped in hot oil. Fry until golden.

Bon appétit!

SERVING: 2 ADULTS, 2 KIDS

Finger Fish

 **TIME: 30 MINS**

These homemade fish fingers are easy, delicious, and a great recipe for kids. These crispy fish fingers can be air-fried and are healthier than store-bought. Put them in a sandwich or just dip them in your kid's favorite sauce.

MATERIAL

- 2 fish fillets, cut into strips 1.5"x4"
- ¼ tbsp parmesan cheese
- 1 cup coarse breadcrumbs/crushed cornflakes
- 1 tbsp mayonnaise
- 1 egg
- 2 pinches of salt
- Pinch of black pepper
- Pinch of paprika
- 2 tbsp all-purpose flour
- Vegetable oil for cooking

CONSTRUCTION

Preheat the oven to 180 degrees. Spread the breadcrumbs on a baking tray and bake for 5 minutes until golden and crisp. Transfer the breadcrumbs to a bowl, add paprika, a pinch of salt, and parmesan, mix well, and set aside.

In another bowl, beat an egg and add mayonnaise, flour, a pinch of salt, and pepper to taste. Give it a good mix. Dip the fish strips in the batter and coat well.

Transfer the coated fish fingers to the breadcrumb bowl and toss well with a spoon.

Heat the cooking oil in a deep frying pan on medium heat. Using tongs, place each fish finger in the frying pan. Don't overcrowd them. Fry on medium heat until fully cooked.

You can also place the coated fish fingers on a baking tray and bake in an oven for 15-20 minutes until well done.

Serve crispy fish fingers with your favorite dip. Bon appétit!

TIP
You can use chicken instead of fish.

SERVING: 2 ADULTS, 2 KIDS

Cauliflower Savory

 TIME: 30 MINS

This recipe is perfect for kids and adults alike. Savory cauliflower is as tasty as can be. Steaming the cauliflower adds so much flavor that you can easily skip the salt when making it for babies or toddlers.

MATERIAL

- 3-4 cups cauliflower florets
- 1 potato, peeled and diced
- 1½ medium tomatoes, sliced
- 1 tbsp crushed garlic
- 3 tbsp fresh coriander leaves, finely chopped
- Pinch of salt and chili powder
- ½ tsp coriander powder
- 3 tbsp cooking oil

CONSTRUCTION

Heat oil in a saucepan over medium heat.

Toss garlic until light brown, add potato, and stir for a few seconds. Add cauliflower, salt, chili powder, and coriander powder and mix well.

Cover with the lid and allow to simmer over low heat. When vegetables are tender, add coriander leaves, stir for a few minutes, and remove from the stove.

Serve with brown rice or chapati.

SERVING: 3 KIDS

Brown Rice

 **TIME: 20 MINS**

Brown rice is seriously delicious, considering it's made with ordinary ingredients. The basic recipe is pretty tasty and satisfying.

MATERIAL

- ½ cup brown rice
- ½ cup frozen mix veggies
- Pinch of salt
- ½ tbsp olive oil
- 3 cups water

CONSTRUCTION

Put oil in a medium saucepan, then add water.

When water boils, add mixed veggies, salt, and rice. Allow to simmer on medium heat until the water has almost gone.

Cover with the lid and steam for 10 minutes on low heat.

Serve with any gravy or chicken stir fry. Bon appétit!

SERVING: 1 ADULTS, 1 KID

Mac and Cheese

 **TIME: 20 MINS**

Macaroni cheese is always a win with children. It is the ultimate comfort food for kids and adults alike. The brilliant thing about this recipe is that it is a healthy mac and cheese because it is packed with hidden veggies.

MATERIAL

- 1 cup whole-grain macaroni
- 2 cups cheddar cheese
- 2 tbsp butter
- ¼ cup plain yogurt
- 2 tbsp all-purpose flour
- Pepper to taste
- ¼ tsp garlic powder
- 1 cup milk
- 1 small carrot or sweet potato, shredded (or any green vegetable)

CONSTRUCTION

Boil the macaroni in a saucepan, drain the water when cooked, and set aside.

While macaroni is cooking, sauté your chosen vegetable in a little olive oil until cooked to your kid's liking, then set aside.

Cheese sauce

Melt the butter in a saucepan, add all-purpose flour, garlic powder, salt, and pepper and mix well. Cook for 1 minute, add milk and mix well. Add plain yogurt and whisk continuously on medium heat until the sauce thickens.

Time to add the cheese and let it melt. Whisk until combined and smooth. (Don't let the sauce boil.)

Add macaroni, mix well, add cooked vegetables, and mix again. Mac and cheese are ready to serve!

TO STORE

Keep in an airtight container in the refrigerator and let your tot enjoy for up to 3 days.

SERVING: 12 SQUARES

Eggless Zucchini Squares

 **TIME: 20 MINS**

These easy eggless zucchini squares are moist, flavorful, and freezer-friendly. Perfect for breakfast, snack, or even lunch.

MATERIAL

- 1 zucchini, shredded
- Pinch of salt and pepper
- 1 tbsp parsley
- 5 tbsp grated cheddar cheese
- 9 tbsp self-raising flour
- 9 tbsp Greek yogurt

CONSTRUCTION

Preheat your oven to 180 degrees.

Squeeze excess water out of shredded zucchini through a clean cloth.

In a bowl, mix all the ingredients well.

Grease a baking tray, or use butter paper, and transfer the mixture to the baking tray.

Bake for 20 to 25 minutes until cooked. Remove from tray and cut into squares.

Serve with your favorite sauce.

Other veggies, such as shredded carrot, sweet potato, or broccoli, can be added.

TO STORE

Keep in an airtight container in the fridge for up to 2 days.

Freezer friendly up to 2 months.

SERVING: 8 NUGGETS

Nuggets

 TIME: 25 MINS

This is a healthy version of chicken nuggets. They are so delicious that they will completely satisfy any baby. Picky eaters will especially love these classic nuggets.

MATERIAL

- 1 chicken breast
- 1 tbsp garlic paste
- ¼ tsp garam masala
- 1 egg
- Pinch of salt
- Breadcrumbs for coating
- Oil for cooking
- Any favorite dip/sauce

CONSTRUCTION

Boil chicken in a saucepan with salt, garlic, and garam masala.

Transfer the cooked chicken to a board, slice, and place in a blender. Add egg and blend until smooth. Add breadcrumbs if sticky. Form shapes from the mixture and coat with breadcrumbs.

Deep fry the chicken nuggets in a frying pan until golden brown.

TO BAKE

Preheat your oven to 180 degrees. Grease a baking tray with butter and place the chicken nuggets on it. Bake for 5-10 minutes, turning once. Remove when crispy.

Asian Spaghetti

SERVING: 2-4 KIDS

TIME: 30 MINS

Another version of spaghetti with Asian spices that everyone loves!

MATERIAL

- ½ chicken breast, finely chopped
- 1 tsp garlic paste
- ½ onion, chopped
- 1 tomato, chopped
- ½ capsicum, chopped
- Pinch of salt
- Pinch of red chili powder
- ¼ tsp garam masala
- ½ tsp coriander powder
- 2 tbsp vegetable oil
- 2 cups spaghetti, broken in half
- 2 tbsp olive oil

CONSTRUCTION

Heat oil in a pan, add onion, and toss until golden brown. Add chicken, stir for a few seconds, add garlic paste, and fry.

Add tomatoes and stir for a few seconds. Cover with the lid for 5-10 minutes over low heat until tomatoes are soft.

Add capsicum, salt, chili powder, coriander powder, and garam masala and cook until oil separates.

Spaghetti

10-15 minutes before the sauce is ready, boil the spaghetti in salty water according to the packet instructions.

Drain the water when cooked and rinse in fresh water to wash out the residue.

Add the boiled spaghetti to the sauce and give it a good mix. Serve hot.

SERVING: 1 ADULT, 1 KID

White Karahi

 **TIME: 30 MINS**

Here is another super easy recipe for your toddler to incorporate protein in their diet without their knowing.

MATERIAL

- 1 chicken breast, cubed
- ¼ tsp garam masala
- 2 tbsp cooking oil
- ¼ cup yogurt
- 1 tsp ginger garlic paste
- ¼ tsp roasted coriander seeds, ground
- ¼ tsp freshly ground black pepper
- ½ tsp roasted cumin seeds, ground
- 2½ tbsp heavy cream
- ½ tbsp unsalted butter
- Pinch of salt

CONSTRUCTION

Heat oil in a wok, add chicken, and fry until golden brown. Add ginger garlic paste and salt and let it cook for 5 minutes on medium heat.

While chicken is cooking, mix yogurt, ground cumin, ground coriander, and black pepper in a bowl.

Transfer the yogurt mixture to the chicken and give it a good mix. Allow the water to evaporate and cook for 5 to 8 minutes until the oil separates on the surface of the curry.

Now add butter and cream, stir for 2 minutes more, and remove from stove. Sprinkle with fresh coriander leaves.

SERVING: 2 ADULTS, 1 KID

Baked Beans

 **TIME: 1HR 30 MINS**

These baked beans are a comforting side dish loaded with protein. They are lower in salt and sugar than the commercial beans available, making them perfect for toddlers.

MATERIAL

- 1 cup white or red beans
- 1 cup chicken broth/vegetable stock (low salt)
- ½ cup water
- 1 tsp Worcestershire sauce
- ¼ tbsp garlic powder
- 1½ tbsp brown sugar
- 3 tbsp ketchup or tomato sauce
- 1 tbsp tomato purée
- ½ tbsp apple cider vinegar
- ¼ tsp black or white pepper
- Pinch of salt
- 4 tsp cornflour

CONSTRUCTION

Soak beans in a big bowl of water overnight. Drain the water and transfer beans to a pot. Add water, cover, and bring to a simmer on high heat.

Skim off the foam that appears on the surface of the water. Reduce the heat and allow to simmer on low-medium heat. Partially cover with the lid to let the steam escape. Cook for 1-2 hours till beans are tender but still firm on the outside. Drain the water. (You can skip this step if you want to cook in a pressure cooker.)

Place all the ingredients, except beans and cornflour, in a pot. Mix well, add beans, and stir.

Allow to simmer on medium heat for 15 minutes uncovered. Stir frequently so the beans don't catch on the bottom of the pot.

Mix the cornflour with ¼ cup of water, add to the beans, and stir for 2-3 minutes until the sauce is thick.

Serve hot, garnished with parsley.

SERVING: 2 KIDS

Fajita

 **TIME: 20 MINS**

Want an easy dinner recipe that you can get cooked and on the table in a matter of minutes? Then this is the recipe for you.

MATERIAL

- 1 chicken breast, diced
- 1 tbsp olive oil
- ½ red bell pepper, cut into strips
- ½ yellow bell pepper, cut into strips
- ½ capsicum, cut into strips
- 2 tsp granulated garlic or garlic powder
- ½ tsp paprika
- 3 tbsp grated cheddar cheese
- Bunch of lettuce, shredded
- 4-5 cherry tomatoes, halved

CONSTRUCTION

Heat oil in a pan, add chicken chunks and garlic powder, and cook for a few seconds.

Add bell peppers and paprika and fry for 5 minutes on medium heat. Make sure the chicken is well-cooked before removing it from the stove.

Serve with lettuce and cherry tomatoes.

SERVING: 2-3 KIDS

Black-eyed Bean Curry

 **TIME: 60 MINS**

Black-eyed bean curry (lobia curry) is quite easy to make. It makes a healthy vegetarian side dish and can be served with rice. It has a unique flavor.

MATERIAL

- ½ cup black-eyed beans or lobia (soaked in water for 6-8 hrs)
- 2 tbsp cooking oil
- 1 onion, chopped
- 1½ tomatoes, chopped
- 1 clove garlic, crushed
- 2 tsp coriander powder
- Pinch of red chili powder
- Pinch of salt
- ½ tsp turmeric powder
- ¼ tsp garam masala
- ½ tsp lemon juice
- Small piece of tamarind
- Pinch of cinnamon powder
- ½ tsp cumin powder
- 1 heaped tbsp fresh coriander leaves

CONSTRUCTION

Heat oil in a pot, add crushed garlic, and toss for a few seconds. Add chopped onion, fry until golden, add tomato, and cook for a minute.

Add coriander powder, turmeric powder, garam masala, chili powder, and cumin powder and mix well. Cook until the oil separates on the surface.

Add beans, 4 cups of water, and salt and allow to simmer on low-medium heat.

Partially cover with the lid, letting the steam escape.

Cook for 35 minutes until the beans are tender and a small quantity of water remains. Stir for few minutes and garnish with fresh coriander leaves.

SERVING: 6 MINI PIZZAS

Mini Pita Pizzas

 **TIME: 25 MINS**

As a light lunch, these mini pizzas are easy to make and use readily available ingredients. The cheeses add to the flavor, and pita bread is the perfect crust.

MATERIAL

- 6 small wholewheat pita bread
- Tomato sauce/ ketchup
- ½ tomato, chopped
- ½ onion, finely sliced
- 6 canned black olives, sliced
- 1 mushroom, chopped
- ¼ capsicum, chopped
- Pinch of dried oregano
- ½ tsp crushed coriander seeds
- 3-4 tbsp shredded mozzarella cheese
- 3-4 tbsp shredded cheddar cheese

CONSTRUCTION

Preheat your oven to 180 degrees.

Spread the tomato sauce on the pita bread and top with your favorite vegetables. Sprinkle with spices and herbs, cover with cheddar and mozzarella, and end with sliced black olives.

Bake for 15-20 minutes in a pre-heated oven until cooked. Bon appétit!

SERVING: 1 ADULT, 1 KID

Chicken Karahi

 TIME: 25 MINS

MATERIAL

- 250g chicken pieces
- 1½ tomatoes, chopped
- 1 tbsp garlic, crushed
- 1 tbsp yogurt
- ¼ tsp white pepper
- ¼ tsp garam masala
- ¼ tsp coriander powder
- ½ tsp ground cumin
- Bunch of fresh coriander leaves, chopped
- Pinch of salt
- 4 tbsp vegetable oil

CONSTRUCTION

Heat oil in a pan, add chicken, and stir for a few minutes over medium heat. Let it cook for 10 minutes until the chicken water has cooked away.

Add tomato, yogurt, and spices and give it a good mix. Cover with the lid for 5-8 minutes until the tomato and chicken are tender.

Stir frequently until the oil separates. Sprinkle coriander leaves on top and serve with chapati or rice.

Fried Fish

SERVING: 2 KIDS

 **TIME: 20 MINS**

MATERIAL

- 1 boneless fish fillet
- 1½ tbsp lime juice
- ½ tsp dried basil
- ¼ tsp dried oregano
- ½ tsp coriander powder
- ½ tsp garlic paste
- ½ tsp paprika
- 2 tbsp olive oil
- Pinch of salt
- Pepper to taste

CONSTRUCTION

In a bowl, mix together lime juice, basil, oregano, coriander powder, black pepper, salt, garlic, paprika, and olive oil.

Apply the mixture to the fish fillet, coating it well on both sides.

Grease a frying pan and fry the fish on high heat for 30 seconds, then reduce the heat and let it cook on medium heat for 4-5 minutes on each side. Remove when golden brown on both sides.

Sprinkle with fresh coriander or parsley. Enjoy!

> **TIP**
> You can also fry the fish in an air fryer.

SERVING: 2 KIDS

Mini Burgers

 TIME: 20 MINS

These mini burgers will best suit older toddlers who are more able to hold and eat them than younger children. However, that doesn't mean that younger children won't enjoy dissecting them and eating each piece separately!

MATERIAL

- 3 mini buns, sliced in half
- 3 tomato slices/cucumber slices
- 3 cheddar cheese squares
- 3 frozen beef or chicken patties (readymade) or chicken nuggets (page 203)
- 3 small lettuce leaves
- Ketchup for spreading and serving
- Mayonnaise for spreading
- Potato fries for serving (optional)

CONSTRUCTION

Fry or grill frozen patties on medium-high heat until cooked.

Microwave or toast buns for 5 minutes on a heated skillet. Spread mayo on all three bottom halves of the buns, then add patties, lettuce leaves, cheddar cheese, ketchup, and sliced tomato and/or cucumber.

Cover each burger with the top of the roll and insert a wooden skewer in the center. Serve with ketchup and fries.

SERVING: 4 PUFFS

Cheese Spinach Puffs

 TIME: 30 MINS

Quick and easy cheese spinach puffs made with simple ingredients. This easy appetizer for babies is crispy with a cheese filling.

MATERIAL

- 4 squares puff pastry, store-bought
- 4 tbsp cooked sausage, evenly diced
- 1 cup fresh spinach, washed and chopped
- ½ cup grated cheddar cheese
- 1 tbsp unsalted butter
- 1 tbsp all-purpose flour
- 2 pinches of black pepper
- ½ cup warm milk
- Pinch of nutmeg (optional)

CONSTRUCTION

Pre-heat your oven to 180 degrees.

Melt butter in a saucepan over medium heat. Add flour and salt and stir frequently until mixture turns golden and slightly aromatic.

Pour in half of the milk and stir constantly, then add the other half of the milk and cook until smooth. Stir on the bottom so the mixture doesn't stick. Cook for about 6 minutes.

Reduce heat to low and let it simmer until sauce thickens. Make sure there are no lumps (otherwise blend it).

Add spinach, black pepper, and nutmeg and stir for 1 minute. Add diced sausages and half the cheddar cheese, mix well, and set aside.

Line a baking tray with wax paper, sprinkle with flour (so the pastry doesn't stick), and arrange the sheets of puff pastry. Pour 1½ tablespoons of the spinach mixture onto each sheet and fold in the corners.

Beat an egg in a small bowl, add water, and mix it to make an egg wash. Brush this over the prepared puffs and bake for 15-20 minutes in the middle of the oven until puffed and golden brown. Serve hot and crisp for lunch or dinner. Bon appétit!

TO STORE

Wrap in parchment paper and keep in an airtight container in the fridge for up to 2 days.

TIP

If in a hurry, fry the spinach in little oil, add garlic paste, a pinch of coriander powder, black pepper, diced sausage, and grated cheddar cheese. Cook until cheese melts and remove from stove. Stuff the store-bought puff pastry with this mixture and pop into the preheated oven for 15 minutes.

Snacks and drinks

SERVING: 6 PIECES

Garlic Bread

 **TIME: 15 MINS**

Try this easy and healthy version of garlic bread suitable for snacks, starters, or a side dish. Amazing flavor – simply brilliant!

MATERIAL

- 6 slices of French bread (1 inch thick)
- 60 g unsalted butter, softened
- 2 garlic cloves, crushed
- 1½ tsp fresh parsley, finely chopped (or Italian mixed herbs to taste)
- 2 to 3 tbsp grated cheddar cheese
- Black pepper to taste

CONSTRUCTION

Pre-heat your oven to 220 degrees (fan-forced)

Mix butter, cheddar cheese, garlic, parsley, and pepper in a bowl. Spread the mixture on each side of the bread.

Bake for 10 to 12 minutes until butter melts and bread gets crispy. Serve hot!

SERVING: 3 KIDS

Hummus

 **TIME: 20 MINS**

This recipe for homemade hummus for babies contains all the ingredients you'd expect to see in the traditional chickpea and tahini dip minus the salt. Perfect for baby-led weaning, toddler snacks, and baby lunches.

MATERIAL

- 2 cups cooked/canned chickpeas
- 1 clove garlic, chopped
- ½ cup tahini paste
- 3 tbsp lemon juice
- Olive oil to drizzle
- 3 ice cubes
- Sumac to sprinkle
- Hot water (if needed)

CONSTRUCTION

Put chickpeas and garlic in a blender and blend for a few minutes. Run at medium speed and add ice cubes, tahini paste, and lemon juice. Blend for a couple more minutes until it reaches your desired consistency.

If it is too thick, add warm water gradually and blend until you achieve a creamy consistency.

Spoon into a small bowl, drizzle with olive oil, and sprinkle with sumac (optional). Serve cold with warm pita bread or cucumber and carrot sticks.

SERVING: 2 KIDS

Fruit Salad

 **TIME: 20 MINS**

The yummiest fruit salad kids will eat, am I right? Easy fruit salad recipes are the best for kids. Here is one for you.

MATERIAL

- 1 apple, diced
- 1 kiwifruit, peeled and chopped
- Handful of any berries
- Bunch of grapes, halved/sliced (or any other fruit you would like to add)
- ½ cup flavored yogurt (vanilla, strawberry, or mango)
- ½ cup chilled, whipped cream

CONSTRUCTION

Place all the fruit in a medium-sized bowl, add yogurt and chilled whipped cream, and mix well. This nutritious fruit salad is ready – delicious!

SERVING: 8-10 SPHERES

Rice Spheres

 **TIME: 10 MINS**

Rice spheres are made with leftover rice and various vegetables as a light and tasty snack.

MATERIAL

- 1 bowl of leftover rice (short or medium grain will stick well)
- 1 potato, boiled and mashed
- Bunch of baby spinach washed and finely chopped
- Pinch of pepper
- Pinch of salt
- ½ tsp coriander powder
- 2 tbsp vegetable oil

CONSTRUCTION

Sauté spinach for a few minutes on medium heat. Transfer the spinach to a bowl and add mashed potato, salt, pepper, and coriander powder. Give it a good mix, add leftover rice, and mix until combined.

Wearing plastic gloves, grease your hand with oil, take a small portion of rice, and form it into a sphere.

Leftover rice spheres are ready as a snack.

TO STORE

You can freeze them for up to 1 month and microwave them before serving.

SERVING: 6 PINWHEELS

Banana Hazelnut Pinwheels

 TIME: 20 MINS

This version of pinwheels would certainly be the highlight of the day. Serve as snacks, put in the lunch box, or take to the party.

MATERIAL

- 1 ready-to-roll puff pastry
- 1 large banana, mashed
- 1 to 2 tbsp hazelnut spread
- 1 egg, beaten for egg wash

CONSTRUCTION

Preheat your oven to 180 degrees. Line a large baking tray with butter paper and set aside.

Sprinkle flour on a clean surface and roll out the puff pastry.

Spread the hazelnut spread lightly across the sheet, then do the same with the mashed banana. Roll tightly and cut in equal slices 2 inches wide. Lie the slices on the baking tray and egg wash to give them a nice glaze. (Do not overcrowd them as pastry needs room to expand.)

Bake for 15 minutes until golden brown. Remove from tray and allow to cool on a wire rack. Pinwheels are ready to serve!

TO STORE

Keep in the freezer in an airtight container for up to 2 months.

SERVING: 1 KID

Sweet Potato Baked Fries

 **TIME: 12 MINS**

Who doesn't love potato fries, but sweet potato fries are simply healthy. These crispy fries are easy to make, kid-friendly, and delicious – the perfect snack for toddlers.

MATERIAL

- 1 sweet potato, peeled and diced
- Pinch of salt (optional)
- Olive oil to drizzle
- 2 tbsp cornstarch
- Black pepper to taste
- ½ tsp coriander powder
- 1 tsp oregano

CONSTRUCTION

Preheat oven to 180 degrees.

Sprinkle salt, cornstarch, and a drizzle of oil on sweet potato cubes and toss well.

Place the fries on a baking sheet and bake for 10 minutes until soft, brown, and crispy.

Transfer fries to a serving bowl, sprinkle with black pepper, coriander powder, and oregano, and enjoy!

SERVING: 8 SPRING ROLLS

Spring Rolls

 TIME: 30 MINS

A sure-shot way to get your kids to eat their vegetables. These spring rolls make excellent snacks for the tiffin box as well.

MATERIAL

- 1 chicken breast, boiled and shredded
- 1 carrot, scrubbed and shredded
- ½ cup spring onions, separated (white and green), finely chopped
- ½ capsicum, finely chopped
- 1 tbsp ginger garlic paste
- ¼ tsp white pepper
- Pinch of salt
- ½ tbsp soy sauce
- Spring roll sheets
- Oil for frying

CONSTRUCTION

Heat oil in a pan over medium heat, add white spring onions, and toss until translucent. Add shredded chicken, carrot, and capsicum and stir well.

Add ginger garlic paste, soy sauce, and spices, fry for few seconds, and add green spring onions. Cook for 2 minutes and remove from the stove. Let the mixture cool for 1 hour at least.

Mix 4 tbsp water with 1 tbsp flour in a small bowl and set aside.

Spoon some stuffing onto each spring roll sheet and roll it up. Coat with the flour mixture and cover the edges.

Deep fry in a pan until golden. Serve with your favorite dip.

Bread Arches

SERVING: 12 MEDIUM BREAD ARCHES

 **TIME: 35 MINS**

MATERIAL

- 3½ cups all-purpose flour
- 1½ cups warm milk or water (not too hot)
- 2 tbsp white or brown sugar
- 1 tbsp active yeast
- Pinch of salt
- 3 tbsp butter
- Grated garlic to sprinkle
- 2 tbsp grated parmesan cheese

CONSTRUCTION

Mix warm milk, sugar, and yeast in a bowl and leave it for 5 minutes to prove.

Add salt and flour to the yeast mixture and knead into a dough. Leave it for 10-15 minutes to rise.

Roll out the dough with a rolling pin into a large square, brush it with melted butter, and sprinkle with cheese. Fold the dough in half. Cut it into 1-inch strips, twist them and shape into arches. Transfer to a cookie sheet or butter sheet on a baking tray. Let them sit for 15 minutes to rise.

Preheat your oven to 180 degrees. Bake for 20 to 25 minutes until light brown. Immediately after baking, sprinkle with garlic salt and cheese.

Serve with your favorite sauce. Bon appétit!

TO STORE

Store in the freezer for up to 2 months and microwave before serving.

> **TIP**
> Halve the recipe if not planning to store.

SERVING: 12 BREAD ROLLS

Bread Rolls

 TIME: 30 MINS

There are many ways to use bread apart from sandwiches, and one such way is with these easy bread rolls.

MATERIAL

- 12 slices of bread without crusts
- ½ cup water
- Oil for cooking

For stuffing

- 1 chicken breast, boiled and shredded
- ½ cup macaroni, boiled
- 3 tbsp grated cheddar cheese (optional)
- ½ tsp black pepper
- ½ tsp Chinese salt
- 1 tbsp soy sauce
- ¼ tsp chili sauce

For coating (optional)

- 1 large egg
- ¾ cup breadcrumbs

CONSTRUCTION

To make stuffing

In a bowl, place shredded chicken, boiled macaroni, spices, and cheese if you want it cheesy.

Mix well until combined. It's okay if the macaroni breaks. You can also add mashed potatoes if you want the mixture to bind well.

Bread rolls

Pour the water into a plate or large bowl. Dip each slice of bread for 1 or 2 seconds, place it on your palm, and press the slice between your hands to drain the excess water. (The bread must stay intact, so press gently.)

Place the damp slice on a plate or board. Put 1 to two scoops of stuffing on the slice and gently roll it up, sealing it on all sides. There should be no exposed stuffing, or it will leak out while frying.

Coating (optional)

Beat an egg in a bowl and place breadcrumbs on a flat plate. Dip the bread roll in beaten egg and roll in breadcrumbs. Dip in the egg again, and dust with breadcrumbs again.

Frying

Place in refrigerator or freezer for 30 minutes to 1 hour before frying. Deep fry or shallow fry in a pan over medium-high heat. Fry until golden brown and cooked inside.

TO STORE

These may be frozen uncooked for up to 2 months. Take out and keep at room temperature for 15 minutes before frying.

SERVING: 2 SANDWICHES

Toasted Sandwiches

 **TIME: 10 MINS**

Toasted sandwiches are kids' favorite. To make healthy sandwiches, rather use wholewheat bread and fill generously with vegetables, eggs, or meat. These sandwiches are easy to make yet filling and delicious as breakfast or a quick evening snack.

MATERIAL

- 4 slices of milk bread or wholewheat bread
- 2 fried or raw potato cutlets (recipe page 169)
- 2 tbsp ketchup
- Vegetable oil for greasing

CONSTRUCTION

Evenly spread the potato cutlet mixture on 2 slices of bread. Add some ketchup if you want, then top with the other 2 slices.

Heat and grease the sandwich maker. Cook according to the instruction manual. (Usually, they take 3-5 minutes to cook.)

Serve with ketchup.

SERVING: 9 SQUARES

Yogurt Cereal Squares

 **TIME: 10 MINS**

Make your own simple yogurt cereal squares for a quick midday snack.

MATERIAL

- 1 cup cereal (any of your favorite cereals)
- 1 cup Greek yogurt or plain yogurt
- 1 tbsp chia seeds

CONSTRUCTION

Whisk the yogurt well. Onto any baking tray (silicone is easy to use), pour out the Greek yogurt ½ inch thick. Sprinkle chia seeds and cereal on top.

Freeze for 12 hours or overnight. Cut into squares, Enjoy!

TO STORE

Keep them in the freezer to enjoy for up to 3 days.

SERVING: 5-6 ROLLUPS

Courgette/Zucchini Rollup

 **TIME: 20 MINS**

An unusual recipe to try, prepared with tomato and courgette.

MATERIAL

- 1 large courgette, finely sliced (lengthwise)
- 1 tomato, chopped
- 2 tbsp coriander leaves
- Pinch of paprika/ black pepper
- Pinch of salt
- ½ tsp coriander powder
- 2 tbsp cooking oil

CONSTRUCTION

Boil water in a saucepan, add courgette slices and a generous amount of salt, and let them simmer for 2 minutes. Lift out the courgette slices one by one with tongs and dip into a bowl of chilled water to stop the cooking process.

Heat oil in a pan, add tomato, black pepper, coriander powder, and salt and mix well. Cover with the lid for 2 minutes over low-medium heat until tomato is tender.

Add coriander leaves and stir on medium heat into a paste. Mix frequently until the oil separates. Remove from stove.

Place 1tbsp of tomato paste on each slice of courgette and roll it up.

Serve with extra tomato paste and garnish with coriander leaves.

SERVING: 6 SQUARES

Rice Krispy Squares

 **TIME: 15 MINS**

A hassle-free recipe with only three ingredients, yet a healthy snack for your little one.

MATERIAL

- 4 tbsp peanut butter (add more if required)
- 4 tbsp maple syrup
- 2 cups Rice Krispies or puffed millet

CONSTRUCTION

Line a 6-inch square baking tray with wax paper and set aside.

Place peanut butter and maple syrup in a microwave-friendly bowl and heat at 20-second increments until warm and fragrant. After 4-5 rounds, the mixture starts to dry and caramelize. (Keep mixing at every turn.)

Add Rice Krispies and mix until well incorporated.

Pour the mixture into a baking tray and spread evenly with a rubber spatula until tightly packed. Freeze for 1 hour, remove, and cut into 8 squares.

Alternatives

Use almond butter or cashew butter and vegan brown rice cereal.

TO STORE

Keep in a cool area or refrigerate in an airtight jar and enjoy for up to 1 week.

SERVING: 5 PUFFS

Potato Puffs

TIME: 25 MINS

Potato puffs are easy to bake, crispy on the outside, soft in the middle, and very scrummy.

MATERIAL

- ½ onion, finely chopped
- ½ tsp cumin seeds, crushed
- 2 medium potatoes, peeled, boiled, and mashed
- ¼ tsp turmeric powder
- ½ tsp coriander powder
- Pinch of black pepper
- ½ tsp garlic paste
- Pinch of salt
- 5 squares puff pastry
- 2 tbsp cooking oil
- 1 egg, beaten, for egg wash

CONSTRUCTION

Preheat your oven to 180 degrees. Line a large baking tray with butter paper and set aside.

Heat oil in a pan over medium heat, toss crushed cumin seeds in the oil, and add garlic and onion. Fry for a couple of seconds until translucent.

Add turmeric powder, black pepper, and coriander powder and mix well. Add mashed potatoes and a pinch of salt to taste. Give it a good mix until combined and remove.

Put some flour on the baking tray so the pastry sheets don't stick. Lay the puff pastry squares on the baking tray and place 2-3 tablespoons of potato stuffing on each. Roll up the sheets and egg wash the tops to get a nice brown glaze.

Place the baking tray in the middle section of the oven and bake for 10 to 15 minutes until golden brown. Remove from oven and allow to cool for a few minutes on a rack. Serve warm, with your favorite dip. Yum!

TO STORE

Store in an airtight container lined with butter paper. Make sure the pasties don't touch each other. Keep in refrigerator for up to 2 days. Warm in microwave or pre-heated oven for a few minutes.

SERVING: 2-3 KIDS

Pasta sticks

 TIME: 30 MINS

Is your kid a pasta lover? Then this recipe is worth trying!

MATERIAL

- 1 cup boiled pasta
- 1 cup mozzarella cheese, grated
- ¼ cup tomato puree
- 2 tbsp ketchup
- ¼ tsp garlic powder
- ¼ tsp oregano
- 1 tbsp chopped tomato
- ¼ cup water
- 1 tbsp chopped capsicum
- ½ tsp chili flakes
- Sliced black olives to garnish

CONSTRUCTION

Pasta sauce

Put tomato puree in a pan on medium-low heat. Add water and mix.

Stir in garlic powder, chili flakes, oregano, and ketchup and mix well. Remove from stove when sauce starts bubbling.

Now thread the pasta onto skewers. Brush some tomato sauce over the pasta, then sprinkle with cheese and garnish with veggies and olives.

Place the skewers in a pan and cover with the lid. Let them cook on low heat. Remove after 10-12 minutes once the cheese has melted. Serve hot!

TO BAKE

Place the pasta sticks in a preheated oven for 5 minutes.

Remove once the cheese has melted.

SERVING: 1 GLASS

Saffron Lassi

 **TIME: 5 MINS**

A healthy drink for your kids in summer!

MATERIAL

- 1 cup curd/yogurt, chilled
- Pinch of saffron strands
- 2 cardamom, ground
- ½ cup chilled water
- 2 tbsp maple syrup (or honey if one year or older)

CONSTRUCTION

Put all the ingredients in a blender or mixer and blend for 2 minutes until well combined.

Adjust sweetness according to your kid's taste, add yogurt if a very thin consistency, or add water if too thick. You can adjust the consistency according to your preference.

Pour into a glass, garnish with saffron strands, and serve cold. Delightful!

Plain White Lassi

SERVING: 1 GLASS

 **TIME: 5 MINS**

MATERIAL

- 1 cup curd/yogurt, chilled
- ½ cup water, chilled
- ¼ tsp (or less) roasted cumin seeds, ground
- Chopped coriander leaves or mint leaves, to garnish
- Pinch of sugar or salt to taste

CONSTRUCTION

Add cumin powder to the curd bowl and mix well. Pour the curd into a blender and add water. Blend it for a couple of seconds until combined and bubbly.

Pour into a glass and garnish with coriander leaves. Serve cold.

SERVING: 1 GLASS

Watermelon Drink

 **TIME: 5 MINS**

A very refreshing drink to beat the scorching heat of summer. Freeze the leftovers and enjoy as an ice-lolly.

MATERIAL

- 1½ cups watermelon, deseeded and chopped
- 1 cup water, chilled
- ½ tbsp lemon juice (optional)
- 1 or 2 tbsp Roohafza/Jam-e-Sherin (syrup or cordial)
- Mints leaves to garnish

CONSTRUCTION

Put all the ingredients in a blender or mixer and blend for a couple of seconds until well combined.

Pour into a glass and garnish with mint leaves. Your summer drink is ready to serve. Yummy!

Double or triple the recipe, make a batch for the whole family, and keep it in the fridge. Serve whenever kids come back inside from the scorching heat.

Apple Cocktail

SERVING: 1 GLASS

 **TIME: 10 MINS**

A nutritious drink, with a bold color, that attracts younger kids to get hydrated after play.

MATERIAL

- 1 apple, cored
- 2 carrots, peeled
- 1 beetroot, peeled
- 1 tbsp maple syrup
  (honey is suitable for a 1-year-old)

CONSTRUCTION

Process all the ingredients in a juicer. Add maple syrup to the juice and stir.

Serve cold or at room temperature. Yummy!

SERVING: 2 GLASSES

Mango Shake

 **TIME: 10 MINS**

The best summer drink. Freeze leftovers into ice lollies. Double or triple the recipe for the whole family.

MATERIAL

- 1 mango, peeled and cut off the pip
- 1½ cups milk
- 2 tbsp maple syrup or 2 tbsp sugar
- 3-4 ice cubes

CONSTRUCTION

Transfer mango flesh to a blender, add maple syrup, and blend for a few seconds. (Sugar needs a couple of minutes to blend.)

Add milk and blend again. Add ice cubes and blend again for a few seconds.

Pour into glasses and serve cold.

TO STORE

Keep in fridge for up to 24 hours or freeze into popsicles and enjoy for up to 1 month.

Treats

SERVING: 8 TRIANGLES

Cake Triangles

 **TIME: 20 MINS**

My mom used to make these for us when we were little. They are easy to make, don't require baking in the oven, and are suitable for evening snacks or lunch boxes.

MATERIAL

- 1 cup all-purpose flour
- 1 cup caster sugar
- ½ cup oil, ghee, or unsalted butter, melted
- 1 egg
- 1 tsp baking powder
- ¼ tsp salt
- ½ tsp vanilla extract
- 2 tbsp cocoa powder (optional)

CONSTRUCTION

Whisk egg in a bowl until bubbly, add sugar, oil, salt, and vanilla and mix well. Fold in flour until well combined and creamy.

Put cocoa in a small bowl, add 3 tablespoons of the prepared mixture, and mix until well incorporated.

Grease the shaped sandwich maker and pour into each cavity 2 to 3 tablespoons of the white mixture and 1 tablespoon of the cocoa mixture on top. Randomly mix with the help of a toothpick.

Cover and cook for 5 minutes according to your sandwich maker instruction manual.

Remove when golden brown. Let it cool for a few minutes, cut in half, and enjoy!

TO STORE

Keep in an airtight bag or container at room temperature. Enjoy for up to 3 days.

SERVING: 10 MINI CHEESECAKES

Eggless Mini Cheesecakes

 **TIME: 35 MINS**

These lip-smacking mini cheesecakes, made without baking, always turn out perfect and creamy. Attempt these for your toddler's little tummy for a special occasion.

MATERIAL

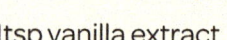

- 2½ cups Lotus or digestive cookie crumbs
- 50g unsalted butter, melted
- 1½ cups mango chunks (fresh or frozen)
- 2¼ cups cream cheese or mascarpone cheese
- ¾ cup caster sugar
- 1tsp vanilla extract
- 150ml heavy cream, whipped
- Fruit to garnish

CONSTRUCTION

Place cookie crumbs in a bowl, add butter, and mix until combined.

Put 1 heaped tablespoon of crumbs in each cavity of a mini cupcake silicone molding tray. Press with the base of a tiny glass until they are tightly packed into a thin layer. Refrigerate while you make the filling.

Blend mango chunks and set them aside. Put cream cheese in a bowl, add caster sugar and vanilla extract, and blend until well combined. Add mango purée to the cream mixture and blend again.

Add whipped cream and blend again until smooth. Remove the molding tray from the refrigerator and pour the cream into the cavities. Level and remove any extra cream with a large knife. Freeze overnight.

Carefully take the mini cheesecakes out of the molding tray and garnish with your favorite topping. Refrigerate before serving.

> **TIP**
>
> Unflavored gelatin powder can be used to make cheesecake stay firm.
>
> Dissolve 1 tbsp gelatin powder in 5 tbsp cold water, let it bloom for 5 minutes, then microwave it for 15 minutes. Add into mango-cream mixture.

Brownie Cubes

SERVING: 6 CUBES

 **TIME: 25 MINS**

MATERIAL

- ½ cup all-purpose flour, sieved
- 5 tbsp cocoa powder, sieved
- ½ tsp baking powder
- ¼ tsp baking soda
- Pinch of salt
- 1 tsp vanilla essence
- ½ cup unsalted butter or ghee, melted
- Two eggs (optional)
- ¾ cup granulated sugar/caster sugar
- Chocolate syrup and sprinkles for topping

CONSTRUCTION

Preheat your oven to 180 degrees for 10 minutes.

Whisk or blend all the ingredients in a glass bowl until the mixture looks like thick chocolate syrup. (Add milk or water if the batter is very thick.)

Line an 8-inch square baking tin with butter paper and grease it. Pour the batter into the baking tin. Place the baking tin on the middle shelf of the oven and bake for 20 minutes.

Remove the baking tin and butter paper, cut into squares, drizzle with chocolate syrup, and decorate with colorful sprinkles or chocolate chips. Your brownies are ready to serve!

SERVING: 8 SWIRLS

Cinnamon Swirls

 TIME: 25 MINS

An occasional treat and something to lift your little one's mood!

MATERIAL

- 1 tbsp ground cinnamon
- 1 sheet of ready-made puff pastry
- ¼ cup granulated sugar
- 2 tbsp unsalted butter
- For icing glaze
- ¼ cup powdered sugar (a more refined form of granulated sugar)
- 1 tbsp unsalted butter
- 1½ tsp vanilla bean paste or vanilla extract
- 3 tbsp milk
- ½ cup mascarpone cheese

CONSTRUCTION

Preheat your oven to 180 degrees.

Unroll the puff pastry sheet on a floured surface so that the pastry doesn't stick.

Combine butter, sugar, and cinnamon in a bowl and brush over the puff pastry. Roll up tightly from the shorter side of the sheet. Slice into 8 even whirls using a bread knife.

Spray or grease the cavities of a muffin tin. Lay each whirl in a cavity and pop the tin on the middle shelf of the oven.

Bake for 10-15 minutes until golden brown. Remove from the tin and allow to cool.

For icing glaze

While the swirls are cooling, mix the mascarpone cheese, sugar, and vanilla in a bowl until smooth. Add butter and mix until well incorporated. Add milk 1 tablespoon at a time and stir until the desired consistency. (Icing should be thick but pourable.)

Place cinnamon swirls on a wire rack. Pour the glaze over the warm cinnamon swirls. Garnish with a pinch of cinnamon. Serve warm!

TO STORE

Keep in a fridge for 3 days in foil or an airtight container. You can also freeze un-glazed swirls and glaze before serving.

TO UNFREEZE

Thaw at room temperature or quickly reheat in the microwave for 2-3 minutes or oven for 10 minutes.

> **TIP**
> Want to skip the icing? Drizzle some ready-made caramel syrup over them.

SERVING: 5 MINI BOWLS

Three-Story Trifle

 TIME: 35 MINS

This yummylicious treat will put a smile on your tot's face! It's a great recipe for parties or special occasions. Prepare a day ahead and appreciate it the next day!

MATERIAL

- 3 tbsp banana custard powder (you can use any)
- 2 cups milk
- ¼ cup cold milk, separate
- 4 tbsp sugar
- 2 small cardamom, ground
- 1 packet jelly powder (any flavor)
- Fruit for topping

CONSTRUCTION

Put custard powder into ¼ cup of milk and make a paste. Set aside.

Boil the 2 cups of milk in a saucepan and add sugar and ground cardamom.

Pour in the custard paste gradually and stir continuously over medium heat until thick and pourable. Remove from stove and let it cool for a few minutes.

Set out the mini bowls and quarter-fill them with the custard. Let it cool at room temperature or refrigerate for 10 minutes.

While custard is cooling, make one packet of jelly according to the instructions. Pour the liquid jelly evenly on the top of the custard and let it set. Place in the refrigerator to speed up the process.

Pour the remaining custard over the jelly and let it cool. Garnish with your kid's favorite fruit.

Chill in the refrigerator, and the family will relish it for up to 2 days!

Energy Bites

SERVING: 12 BITES

 **TIME: 15 MINS**

Boost your kid's and your immunity by having these incredible date bites.

MATERIAL

- ½ cup rolled oats/instant oats
- ½ cup pistachios or almonds (you can use any dry fruit)
- ½ cup desiccated coconut
- 1 cup dates, pitted

CONSTRUCTION

Put all the ingredients in a blender or food processor and blend until well combined.

Knead and form into the desired shape. Healthy snacks are ready.

TO STORE

Keep in an airtight jar and enjoy for up to a week.

SERVING: 3-4 POPSICLES

Popsicles

 **TIME: 15 MINS**

Did you say summer is here? These fruity, healthy popsicles are perfect to cool your tots down from the scorching heat.

MATERIAL

- 1 cup strawberry chunks (any fruit, such as berries or kiwifruit can be used)
- ½ cup maple syrup (you can add more)
- 1 tbsp lemon juice (optional)
- ½ cup water

CONSTRUCTION

Blend all the ingredients in a food processor or blender. Pour the mixture into a popsicle mold and freeze overnight. Enjoy the next day!

(You can double the recipe if more are required.)

***It is safe for a 6-month-old teething baby.**

Golden Popsicles

MATERIAL

- 1 large apple skinned, cored, and diced
- 2 peaches, peeled and stoned
- 4 to 5 dried apricots
- 2 tbsp maple syrup

CONSTRUCTION

Steam apple chunks for about 10-15 minutes and cook on low heat until tender.

Transfer tendered apple chunks, maple syrup, peach flesh, and dried apricot in a blender. Purée until smooth. Pour out in popsicles mold and freeze it overnight. Eat whenever your kids crave, yummy!!

*It is safe for a 6-month-old teething baby.

SERVING: 6 MUFFINS

Banana Muffins

 **TIME: 30 MINS**

Who doesn't like muffins? Try these tempting banana muffins with your kids. You can actually involve your kids in helping you. I'm sure they'll enjoy making them.

MATERIAL

- 3 bananas, very ripe and mashed
- ½ tbsp vanilla powder or 1 tbsp vanilla extract
- 1 egg
- 1½ cups all-purpose flour
- ¾ cup brown sugar
- 3 tbsp milk
- ¼ cup oil or unsalted butter, melted
- 1½ tsp baking soda
- ¼ tsp salt
- Crushed dried fruit (optional)
- White melted chocolate to garnish

CONSTRUCTION

Preheat your oven to 220 degrees. Line a muffin tin with paper cups and set aside.

In a large mixing bowl, place ripe banana, egg, milk, oil, and vanilla extract (if using the liquid form). Whisk together well.

Pour the flour, sugar, and dried fruit on top of the mixture. Add salt and baking soda. Whisk with a hand whisk or hand blender until smooth. The batter should be thick but pourable.

Pour the batter into each muffin cavity, filling it to the rim. Place the tin in the middle section of the oven and bake for 20-25 minutes until dusky golden brown. Insert a toothpick and make sure it comes out dry.

Let them cool for few minutes, then remove them from the muffin tin. Garnish with melted chocolate or serve with strawberry jam.

You can invite your kids to help you decorate the muffins. Kids love such activities and quickly get involved.

Melted chocolate

Pour some water into a saucepan and let it simmer on low-medium heat.

Put a glass bowl on the top of the saucepan, making sure it doesn't touch the water. Add the chocolate and stir frequently until the chocolate melts and there are no lumps.

Pour into a piping bag and garnish.

TO STORE

Keep in an airtight container, wrapped in a paper towel to prevent them from getting soggy. Keep in the fridge for up to 3 or 4 days.

> **TIP**
>
> If you want to melt chocolate in the microwave, put the chocolate in a bowl and microwave for 15 to 20 seconds. Give it a little stir and microwave again for 15 seconds. Whisk again and put in the microwave for 10 seconds. If not completely melted, microwave for a couple of seconds more.

SERVING: 10 COOKIES

Healthy Eggless Cookies

 **TIME: 30 MINS**

These eggless cookies are equally yummy and healthy for your little ones to try. Make a batch and serve whenever they crave them!

MATERIAL

- 1 cup whole grain flour, sieved
- 1 cup old-fashioned oats, sautéed and ground
- ½ cup unsalted butter, melted
- 3 tbsp milk
- ¼ tsp salt
- ½ cup jaggery powder or brown sugar sieved (sieving is important)
- ¼ tsp ground cinnamon
- ¼ tsp ground cardamom
- ½ tsp baking powder
- 3-4 tbsp crushed nuts, chocolate chips, or dried fruit (optional)

CONSTRUCTION

Preheat the oven to 180 degrees. Line a large baking tray with baking paper and set aside.

In a large bowl, mix together flour, oats, cinnamon, cardamom, and salt.

In another bowl, beat together the soft butter and sieved jaggery powder until creamy. Add milk and stir in. Transfer to the bowl with the flour mixture and add crushed nuts. Mix well until combined into a sticky dough.

Roll a small portion of the dough into a ball. Flatten it between your palms to make a circle and place on the baking sheet. Repeat with the remaining dough. (Don't overcrowd the baking tray. Leave a 2-3-finger gap between the unbaked cookies.)

Bake for 15 to 20 minutes or a little longer if you want them crispy. Remove from the oven, allow to cool for few minutes, then transfer to a wire rack. Chow down!

TO STORE

When cool, store in an airtight jar and let your kids enjoy healthy cookies for up to a week. Serve with a cup of milk.

SERVING: 6-8 SHOOTERS

Oreo Shooters

 **TIME: 20 MINS**

A super-duper easy and scrumptious recipe to make for birthday parties and other occasions. Make a day ahead and enjoy the next day.

MATERIAL

- 8 Oreo cookies
- 1½ cups mascarpone cheese, softened
- ½ cup chilled heavy cream, whipped
- 1 tsp vanilla extract
- ½ cup powdered sugar
- Oreo cookies to garnish

CONSTRUCTION

For base

Grind Oreo cookies into crumbs. Put a tablespoon of cookie crumbs into each shooter glass. Press down well so they stick together. Refrigerate while making the filling.

For filling

Whip cream in a bowl until thick and set aside. In another bowl, mix mascarpone cheese, vanilla extract, and powdered sugar until well incorporated.

Fold the whipped cream into the mascarpone mixture and stir well. Crush some more Oreo cookies and add to the filling mixture. Fold in with a spatula.

Transfer the filling to a piping bag and pipe it evenly into each shooter glass. (You can also put the filling in a plastic Ziplock bag, trim one corner about ½ inch, and pipe out the filling like that.)

Garnish with broken Oreo cookies. Serve cold!

9 months to 12 months

Schematic Weekly Planner

week 1

	DAY 1	DAY 2	DAY 3	DAY 4	DAY 5	DAY 6	DAY 7
EARLY MORNING	Breast/formula milk	Breast/formula milk	Breast/formula milk	Breast/formula milk	Breast/formula milk	Breast/formula milk	Breast/formula milk
BREAKFAST	Egg muffins	Boiled egg puffs	Cheese egg toast	Cereal with milk	Textured omelete	Chaffle squares	Mango french toast pyarmid
LUNCH	Easy peasy pasta	Chicken gravy with rice/roti	Cauliflower savory with rice/roti	Finger fish	Eggless zucchini squares	Mutton brown with roti	Aloo paratha sheets
SNACKS	Sweet potato fries	Leftover rice spheres	Energy bites	Spring rolls	Fruit salad	Yogurt cereal squares	Humus with pita bread
DINNER	Breast/formula milk	Breast/formula milk	Breast/formula milk	Breast/formula milk	Breast/formula milk	Breast/formula milk	Breast/formula milk

week 2

	DAY 1	DAY 2	DAY 3	DAY 4	DAY 5	DAY 6	DAY 7
EARLY MORNING	Breast/formula milk	Breast/formula milk	Breast/formula milk	Breast/formula milk	Breast/formula milk	Breast/formula milk	Breast/formula milk
BREAKFAST	Brown rice cereal	Tomato egg savory	Paratha swirls	Cereal breams	Fritatas	Bread pizza	Pancake donuts
LUNCH	Lentil soup	Potato cutlets	Broccoli pasta	Brown rice with veggies	Chicken nuggets	Aloo palak	Falafel with rice
SNACKS	Garlic bread	Flavored yogurt	Potato coils	Banana puff pastry	Sandwich	Bread roll	Fruit salad
DINNER	Cheese spheres	Cheese spinach puffs	White karahi	Chicken croquette	Lobia curry	Zucchini fritters	Finger fish

*Maintain the usual milk intake during the night.

Acknowledgments

By the grace of God, this book has finally reached completion. It's been a long journey, exciting, tough, and quite challenging. I never imagined that I would be creating food plates rather than skyscrapers. Yet my son, Zia, caused me to explore another side of me. This book exists because of him. I drained all my energy making it a reality. I'm grateful for the constant support I had from my life partner, Moiz. I've made it this far only because of him. I'm truly thankful to my parents, especially my mom, who taught me how to cook and how to present food.

I would like to express my deepest gratitude to Ms. Manjri Saxena, my photographer, who worked with me day and night on this journey and took such incredible photos; they give life to this book. You will find her on Instagram under the handle @manjrisaxena.

Thanks a bunch to my lovely sister, Samra, and Jaweria(java), my dearest buddy. They both accelerated my speed when I had writer's block. My friends and my Insta-family who kept me motivated and were ready to offer help if I needed any. Warda, for helping me to lay the first stone of this book. Finally, yet importantly, I want to thank the team of Publishing Push who assisted me in publishing my cookery book and gave this book a physical form.

Index for recipes

A

Aloo Paratha Mini Sheets 174

Apple 71

Apple Cocktail 263

Apple Oats Puree 95

Apple Peaches Apricot 79

Asian Spaghetti 204

B

Baked Beans 208

Banana 71

Banana Hazelnut Pinwheels 235

Banana Muffins 283

Belgian Chocolate Chip Waffles Squares 137

Blackberries 71

Black Eyed Bean Curry 213

Boiled Egg Puff Pastry Pockets 126

Bread Arches 240

Bread Pizza 148

Bread Rolls 242

Broccoli Pasta 181

Broccoli Potato Blend 81

Brown Rice 197

Brown Rice Cereal 157

Brownie Cubes 273

C

Cake Triangles 268

Carrot 68

Cauliflower Savory 195

Cereal Energy Bars 161

Chaffle Squares 141

Cheese Egg Toast 143

Index for recipes

Cheese Spheres 184
Cheese Spinach Puffs 222
Chicken Croquettes 164
Chicken Gravy 189
Chicken Karahi 217
Chicken Nuggets 203
Chicken Skewers 171
Chickpeas and Carrot Blend 93
Chinese Fried Rice 176
Cinnamon Swirls 274
Cooked Oats 111
Courgette/Zucchini Roll Up 249
Crepe 144

D

Double Decker Jammie Dodger French Toast 125
Dragon Fruit and Peach 83

E

Easy Peasy Pasta 179
Egg Mince 151
Egg Muffins 147
Egg Paratha Roll 159
Egg Roll 154
Eggless Mini Cheesecakes 270
Eggless Zucchini Squares 201
Energy Bites 279

F

Fajita 211
Falafel Spheres 191
Finger Fish 192
French Toast Bars 104
Fried Fish 219
Frittata 132
Fruit Chia Pudding 97
Fruit Salad 231

G

Garlic Bread 227
Golden Popsicles 282

H

Healthy Eggless Cookies 286
Humus 229

Index for recipes

L

Lemon Vanilla Waffle Squares 139

Lentil Soup 167

M

Mac and Cheese 198

Mango 70

Mango Shake 265

Mango Toast Pyramid 122

Mini Burgers 221

Mini Pita Pizza 215

Mutton Brown 186

O

Oreo Shooters 288

Overnight Oats 135

P

Pancake Mini Donuts 152

Papaya 70

Parsnip 69

Pasta Sticks 254

Peach 70

Peach Blackberry Chia Puree 89

Peach Chia Pudding 87

Pea and Sweet Potato 85

Peas 69

Pink Pancake Pile 129

Plain White Plain Lassi 259

Popsicles 281

Potato Carrot Rice Puree 99

Potato Cutlets 169

Potato Puff 252

Potato Spinach Savory 183

R

Rice Cereal 72

Rice Krispy Squares 251

Rice Spheres 233

S

Sabu Dana/Sago/Tapioca Pearl Cereal 73

Saffron Lassi 257

Scrambled Egg 109

Semolina (Soji) Cereal 72

Spinach Eggy Bars 117

Index for recipes

Spinach Omelet Swirls 107
Spinach Sweet Potato Blend 91
Spring Rolls 239
Swede 69
Sweet Potato 68
Sweet Potato Baked Fries 237

T

Textured Omelet 131
Three Story Trifle 276
Toasted Sandwiches 245

V

Vegan Banana Oat Pancakes 112
Vegan Zucchini Squares 114

W

Watermelon Drink 261
White Karahi 207

Y

Yogurt Cereal Squares 247

Z

Zucchini and Pea Porridge 101
Zucchini Fritters 173

About the author

Sanya is a certified architect and passionate homemaker who moved from Pakistan to Qatar in 2018. She has certification in child nutrition and cooking. She loves modern architecture, design, and event management. She claims that she is a creative soul and compassionate by nature.

She is a mommy influencer and has an Instagram channel named "mom4amdoha" where she shares primarily about parenting, baby-mama styling, and her baby-led-weaning journey with her son Zia. The success of their BLW lifted her spirits and inspired her to compile all her BLW recipes into this cookbook.

Being from an architectural background, Sanya understands the importance of a strong foundation, even for a baby-led-weaning structure. She hopes this baby cookbook offers tremendous help to mommies, daddies, and caregivers and makes their BLW journey enjoyable.

About the author

To catch a glimpse of her mom-life, you'll find her on Instagram under the handle @mom4amdoha.

For more, visit her website: **www.mom4amdoha.com**.

MOM4AMDOHA

www.ingramcontent.com/pod-product-compliance
Lightning Source LLC
Chambersburg PA
CBHW051309110526
44590CB00031B/4355